T0049077

"This book isn't just about Epiphany; it is filled with epiphanies. In the way only she can, Fleming Rutledge points us anew to the glory of Christ with insight after insight. Thanks to this book, even this low-church evangelical will mark Epiphany this year and, more importantly, will be reminded all year of the way God speaks to us in both the mysterious and the ordinary."

Russell Moore, editor in chief of *Christianity Today*

"There is no one better to introduce the little-understood church season of Epiphany than Fleming Rutledge. This book is a gift—not only for those who belong to traditions that closely observe the church calendar but also for those who may not. Rutledge's love for Epiphany shines throughout, not least because she elucidates its biblical foundations and edifying purpose for the church. Most importantly, Rutledge gets to the heart of the matter—Epiphany is a celebration of the gospel, the season unfolding the manifestation of God's revelation in Christ, of 'God's definitive and unique actions in the One who has been born in Bethlehem.'"

Kimlyn Bender, professor of Christian theology at George W. Truett Theological Seminary, Baylor University

"One of first women to be ordained in the Episcopal Church, Fleming Rutledge has had a fruitful career of teaching preachers to communicate the gospel for the formation of the flock in love of God and neighbor. In this volume, Dr. Rutledge focuses on the liturgical season of Epiphany. Incorporating close readings of Scripture (both Greek and Hebrew texts) and Anglican prayers and hymns, she leads us week by week through Epiphany, showing how this season among any other most fully manifests the glory of God in the face of Jesus Christ. This book joins Dr. Rutledge's other books as a blessing to the church."

Kathryn Greene-McCreight, priest affiliate at Christ Church New Haven and author of *Galatians: A Theological Commentary*

"In *Epiphany*, Fleming Rutledge shows how recovering a delight in the glory of God in Jesus Christ is 'needed by the church right now as a drowning person needs a lifeboat.' Written with joyful urgency yet patient wisdom, this book should be required reading for pastors seeking to recover the wonder of Epiphany. Veterans and newcomers to celebrating the liturgical year will find a treasure of biblical and theological insight in this succinct yet potent work. Moreover, anyone who aches for an alternative to the empty 'glories' so widely pursued today will be nourished by this exposition of the strange yet beautiful reality of God's resplendent glory, displayed in the crucified Lord."

J. Todd Billings, professor of theology at Western Theological Seminary and author of *The End of the Christian Life*

"With palpable reverence and predictable erudition, Fleming Rutledge unearths the riches of the most overlooked season of the liturgical year. Epiphany is all about glory, chiefly the glory of the person of Christ revealed in majesty and power as the King of the Jews and Lord of the Gentiles in key moments of the biblical drama. In Epiphany and the season leading up to Lent, the church gathers a fresh chance to behold the glory of her Lord and to renew itself in the work of proclaiming his glory to the world."

Katelyn Beaty, journalist and author of *Celebrities for Jesus*

Fleming Rutledge

Esau McCaulley, SERIES EDITOR

Epiphany

The Season of Glory

Fullness of Time series

An imprint of InterVarsity Press
Downers Grove, Illinois

InterVarsity Press
P.O. Box 1400 | Downers Grove, IL 60515-1426
ivpress.com | email@ivpress.com

Cover design: David Fassett
Interior design: Daniel van Loon
Image credits: Getty Images: © Warmworld, © OllgaP, © Anne Antonini / EyeEm,
          © lasagnaforone, © mycola

ISBN 978-1-5140-0038-0 (print) | ISBN 978-1-5140-0039-7 (digital)

Printed in the United States of America ⊖

Library of Congress Cataloging-in-Publication Data
A catalog record for this book is available from the Library of Congress.

29 28 27 26 25 24 23 | 11 10 9 8 7 6 5 4 3 2 1

For Elizabeth

who, at the crucial moment, gave me the gift of
uninterrupted time for writing.
Dedicated in faith, hope, and love.

Contents

The Fullness of Time
Series Preface by Esau McCaulley – *1*

Author's Preface – *3*

Introduction – *7*

1
The Glory – *19*

2
The Day – *47*

3
The Season – *53*

4
The Star – *58*

5
The River – *73*

6
The Wine – *90*

7
The Ministry – *98*

8
The Teaching – *108*

9
The Mountain – *119*

10
The Mission – *132*

Coda: Doxology – *141*

Notes – *151*

The Fullness of Time

SERIES PREFACE

ESAU McCAULLEY, SERIES EDITOR

Christians of all traditions are finding a renewed appreciation for the church year. This is evident in the increased number of churches that mark the seasons in their preaching and teaching. It's evident in the families and small groups looking for ways to recover ancient practices of the Christian faith. This is all very good. To assist in this renewal, we thought Christians might find it beneficial to have an accessible guide to the church year, one that's more than a devotional but less than an academic tome.

The Fullness of Time project aims to do just that. We have put together a series of short books on the seasons and key events of the church year, including Advent,

Christmas, Epiphany, Lent, Easter, and Pentecost. These books are reflections on the moods, themes, rituals, prayers, and Scriptures that mark each season.

These are not, strictly speaking, devotionals. They are theological and spiritual reflections that seek to provide spiritual formation by helping the reader live fully into the practices of each season. We want readers to understand how the church is forming them in the likeness of Christ through the church calendar.

These books are written from the perspective of those who have lived through the seasons many times, and we'll use personal stories and experiences to explain different aspects of the season that are meaningful to us. In what follows, do not look for comments from historians pointing out minutiae. Instead, look for fellow believers and evangelists using the tool of the church year to preach the gospel and point Christians toward discipleship and spiritual formation. We pray that these books will be useful to individuals, families, and churches seeking a deeper walk with Jesus.

Author's Preface

In the 1940s, when I was very young, my mother occasionally took me with her as she did her regular stint as a member of the altar guild in our tiny Episcopal church in Tidewater Virginia. The calendar of the church year always hung on the wall of the sacristy, in a format that can still be seen today in some parishes. All the days of the year were shown in their proper liturgical colors, and it was cheerful to look at. Epiphany was green. That calendar fascinated me as a child. It was a visual companion to my mother's reverent altar work and my grandmother's King James Bible. All my life I have found the liturgical calendar to be a primary source of identity, belonging, and delight. I am therefore grateful to be able to make this contribution to a new series about the seasons of the church year. It is intended not for academic specialists, but for anyone: pastors, church musicians, teachers, worship leaders, students, inquirers, anyone at all who wants to deepen their understanding of a rich and ancient heritage—or to begin to learn it for the first time.

A great many Christians have not been nurtured in the church's calendar, except for the more or less universally recognized holidays of Christmas and Easter. This lacuna in Christian heritage is beginning to be replenished rather unexpectedly. Groups of Protestants with no experience of the liturgical year have begun to show a marked interest in it. This phenomenon is most welcome. It is part of a renewal of interest in the patristic and medieval periods generally, and in the many treasures to be found in some of the traditions that were discarded after the Reformation. I am very much a Reformed Protestant thinker myself, so I am hoping that this book will appeal to those who have not been immersed in the more catholic traditions.

This exciting new phenomenon of inquiry and experimentation comes with a caveat, however. Many worshiping communities have enthusiastically taken up using the ancient calendar as though it were an easy thing to accomplish—as though lighting an Advent wreath (a *very* recent development) and releasing balloons on the Day of Pentecost (ditto) would do the trick almost overnight. On the contrary, understanding and enacting the seasons in their depths requires patient learning and substantial immersion. A superficial Advent, in particular, may be worse than no Advent at all, because it passes so lightly over the apocalyptic depths of the season. Nor does Epiphany—the subject of this book—yield its wonders easily. Entering into and receiving the riches of the liturgical cycle requires humility and patience. Above all, a willingness to "read, mark, learn, and inwardly digest"[1] the *biblical* foundations of the seasons is essential, and that cannot be done in a few weeks, or by glancing over a few notes in a weekly bulletin. Full immersion is necessary, and that can happen only with embodied commitment over periods of years—two or three years to begin with, and a lifetime to absorb and make one's own.

This little book, however, cannot pretend to be anything other than one small offering along the way of reinvigorating the church's way of thinking about seasonal observance. If these pages can be of any small help in the major project of reorienting the people of God to live according to the seasonal rhythms of the story of redemption, that will indeed be a cause for thanksgiving.

The message of "Jesus Christ and him crucified" (1 Corinthians 2:2), unfolded year by year in the church's calendar, is life itself. In this modest attempt to suggest the depths and wonders of the Epiphany season, even from the confines of age and restricted mobility, I have been consoled and encouraged by the promise in the concluding words of the Proper Preface for the Feast of the Epiphany:

> Through Jesus Christ our Lord; who in substance of our mortal flesh, manifested forth his glory; that he might bring us out of darkness into his own glorious light.[2]

Amen.

Fleming Rutledge
Rye Brook, New York
Ash Wednesday 2022

Introduction

M any scholars have attempted to reconstruct the earliest years of the liturgical calendar. It is pleasing to imagine the leaders of the emerging Christian communities discussing the various portions of the Bible and attaching them to the various liturgical feasts and seasons, selecting which ones to use and how to place them in a sequence. Exactly how all of this was accomplished in the first four centuries is largely unrecoverable to historical method. The wonder is that still today, the liturgical calendar retains its power. The list of historical calamities over the centuries has been amplified by the extreme, indeed unprecedented, global threats of our own time in the third millennium, and yet the Word of God read in the sequence of the church seasons remains ever "living and active, sharper than any two-edged sword" (Hebrews 4:12). Whatever charges can be brought against the lectionary, it remains an extraordinary sword in the hands of the Church Militant.[1]

We know for certain that the liturgical calendar began to take shape in the first four centuries AD, but it did not become embedded in all formal Christian worship until the sixteenth century. When the Protestant Reformation declared its independence from the Church of Rome, a large part of the Western church abandoned the calendar, along with a great many other accumulated traditions. Observation of the church seasons remained largely intact, however, in the Anglican Communion (including American Episcopalians), the Lutheran church, the Moravian church, and a few other smaller branches. In recent decades, there has been a phenomenal resurgence of interest in the other American "mainlines"— Methodists, Presbyterians, Congregationalists, the Reformed churches—and also in a surprising number of looser forms of Protestantism.

This somewhat unexpected development has shown that the calendar can be a powerful aid to growth in faith and service. The rhythm of the seasons, the repetition of the sequence year after year despite outward circumstances, the variety and richness of the Scripture readings, and, most of all, the story that the seasons tell in narrative progression throughout the year—all of this can be powerful for the nourishment of growth in grace. Thus we may say that the calendar is *edifying*—providing instruction, guidance, and inspiration for the upbuilding of the church.

But above all, the church year leads us to Jesus Christ. This will be the central focus of the pages that follow. The progression of seasons, when all is said and done, is designed so that the members of Christ's body may participate even now in his eternal life by rejoicing in his living presence, following him in our various vocations, enacting his teachings in our ministries, knowing him as our Savior, and above all glorifying him as Lord. In our time, however, many of the very same mainline churches who show a new interest in the church seasons have grown weak in proclaiming Christ. It does not give me any pleasure to note this. Jesus of Nazareth is revered as a teacher and moral exemplar, not infrequently side by side with various other religious figures, but the apostolic message about the unique identity and destiny of the Messiah (*Christos*) has become attenuated. As for the so-called evangelical, conservative, or right-wing churches, they have often allowed Jesus to become a repository of various grievances, so that the invocation of his name at political rallies has become commonplace. When something or someone less than God in Jesus Christ is evoked in worship, the central focus of the apostolic message is obscured, if not negated outright.

The good news that the Scriptures proclaim will not thrive in this theological crisis. Serious attention paid to the themes of the season following the Feast of the Epiphany, in particular, can be a strong antidote to a weak Christology. To be sure, all of the church calendar is formed around Jesus, but there is a sense in which Epiphany is the most specifically christological season.[2] The lectionary readings for Epiphany are chosen and arranged in an order designed to glorify him. When the season is preached and taught with this in mind, there can be no doubt—for those who have ears to hear—as to who Jesus is and what he has been born to accomplish. As we shall see, there are particular events from Christ's life that have been part of Epiphany for two millennia—events that specifically elevate him as Savior and Lord.

Because of this, the season needs to be brought into the foreground along with Christmas. If the season of

Epiphany were to be strongly presented as a central, cohesive narrative during the winter months by clergy, teachers, and other leaders, it would make a powerful impression. Lent gets more attention, and for good reason, but Epiphany can excel in theological and narrative power if it is forcefully shaped, preached, and taught. If those who shape worship in local congregations took seriously the opportunity to manifest the identity, mission, and, yes, the glory of Christ as Epiphany unfolds, it could be a transformative season of growth in faith. It is not for nothing that the season has been associated with mission and growth—with the spread of the gospel (much more of that later).

The season of Epiphany always begins on January 6 (the Feast of the Epiphany) and extends until Ash Wednesday, the beginning of Lent. Ash Wednesday's date is determined by the date of Easter, so Epiphany is much shorter in some years than in others. This may have something to do with its comparative neglect in the church.[3] Despite its beauty and depth, it is arguably the least understood and least appreciated of all the seasons. We know Advent, or think we do, because it comes just before Christmas—a fact which, for better and worse, has shaped the season.[4] We know that Lent means the cross, and

Easter means the empty tomb. Pentecost means the descent of the Spirit.[5] Epiphany means . . . what, exactly?

Epiphaneia in New Testament Greek means *manifestation.* An effective method of teaching the content of the faith, not often enough used, is to instruct congregations in the texts of the seasonal hymns. This can be easily done by calling attention to the words being sung in the service of worship. One of the Epiphany hymns, "Songs of Thankfulness and Praise," which briefly summarizes the trajectory of the season, repeats the word "manifest" a number of times, so as to make clear its significance. This hymn text displays the major biblical passages associated with Epiphany in narrative order.[6] It remarkably sets out the Epiphany sequence in order of its special themes:

> Manifest at Jordan's stream,
> Prophet, Priest, and King supreme;
> And at Cana, wedding guest,
> In thy Godhead manifest;
> Manifest in pow'r divine,
> Changing water into wine;
> Praises be to thee addressed,
> God in flesh made manifest.

Manifest in making whole
Palsied limbs and fainting soul;
Manifest in valiant fight,
Quelling all the devil's might;
Manifest in gracious will,
Ever bringing good from ill;
Praises be to thee addressed,
God in flesh made manifest.

Following this striking summary, the Episcopal hymnal inserts a verse by the noted clergyman F. Bland Tucker, in order to complete the sequence with the climactic scene of the transfiguration:[7]

Manifest on mountain height
Shining in resplendent light,
Where disciples filled with awe
Thy transfigured glory saw.
When from there thou leddest them
Steadfast to Jerusalem;
Cross and Easter Day attest,
God in man made manifest.

Each of these references in the hymn refers to passages in Scripture that "manifest" the identity of Jesus as God in human form. They are "epiphanies"—events of revelation not available to human beings without an act of God. This is important, because in biblical faith, knowledge of the true God is not attainable by human effort. We cannot summon up the presence of the living Jesus by efforts of our own, however "spiritual"; his presence is his to give.[8] Any manifestation that reveals Jesus' true identity occurs because the power of God is at work upon the eyes, ears, and hearts of the recipients. The unfolding of the Epiphany season is therefore a record of God's definitive and unique actions in the One who has been born in Bethlehem.

We may therefore note that the familiar Christmas hymn of Charles Wesley, "Hark! The Herald Angels Sing," sets out in one verse a capsule of Nicene doctrine:

Christ, by highest heaven adored,
Christ, the everlasting Lord . . .
veiled in flesh the Godhead see;
hail th'incarnate Deity,
pleased with us in flesh to dwell,
Jesus, our Emmanuel.

The fulness of the incarnation that has taken place will be manifested in various ways during the Epiphany season—and climactically in Lent and Easter soon to follow. The themes of Epiphany can be powerfully preached and taught for the health and growth of the church. They are revelatory themes, suitable to the overall motif of *manifestation* or *showing forth*—the basic definition of *epiphaneia* in New Testament Greek. What exactly is it that is shown forth? We shall see as the biblical witness unfolds.

A WORD ABOUT THE LECTIONARY

Various Sunday lectionaries have been used over the centuries, but for the purposes of this series on the church seasons it is important to note that many of its prominent seasonal passages have been in place since the very earliest centuries—particularly those for the major themes of Epiphany described in these pages. The most commonly used lectionary at present in the American Protestant denominations is the Revised Common Lectionary (RCL), which has strong roots in the post-Vatican II Roman Catholic lectionary. The RCL was authorized in 1992 for use in the Episcopal Church as a replacement for the Common Lectionary (CL), which can still be found at the back of the 1979 Book of Common Prayer.

Despite its widespread use, the RCL has proven controversial. One of its improvements over the CL was supposed to be a greater emphasis on the Old Testament, with longer sequential passages, sometimes spread over many Sundays. This has been a mixed blessing. It can be argued that it has resulted in less, rather than more, preaching from the Old Testament. The CL brought Old Testament passages into conversation with the New Testament in ways that illuminated them both. In two decades of Sunday preaching before 1992, I found this to be of inestimable advantage. I have therefore based this book on the earlier (1983) Common Lectionary.

AND ABOUT TRANSLATIONS

The King James Version (KJV), for me, remains the gold standard of the English language. There is no way adequately to calculate its influence on the best writing and speech over many centuries. It should be emphasized that the preaching of the Black church would not have been the inspired influence that it has been without the KJV. (I can still hear Fannie Lou Hamer saying about her persecutors during the struggle for the Mississippi vote, "They know not what they do."[9]) I urge readers to read and use the KJV from time to time. I continue to prefer to use the Revised Standard Version (RSV) in my books because, although it is modernized, it retains at least some of the cadence of the KJV (for example, "As in Adam all die, so also in Christ shall all be made alive" [1 Corinthians 15:22]). However, I have occasionally quoted the New Revised Standard Version, New International Version, and others; these departures from the RSV are noted in parentheses.

I

The Glory

The Feast of the Epiphany on January 6 once had an alternative title. Pope Leo I ("Leo the Great") referred to it in his Homilies not as *Epiphaneia* but as *Theophania*—a manifestation *of God* (*theos*). The famed "Tome of Leo" became a conclusive statement of orthodox Christology when it was ratified at the Council of Chalcedon in AD 451, and it remains today a christological gold standard for anyone seeking a clear statement of Jesus Christ's person as *theophany*.[1]

We will approach the season of Epiphany (or theophany) by focusing on just one word: *glory*. The season following January 6 begins, continues, and comes to a climax with various *epiphanies* of the glory of Jesus Christ as the only begotten Son of God. A good place to begin is one verse from the prologue of the Gospel of John, one of the most important testimonies to the identity of Jesus in all of Scripture, and certainly a foundation for orthodox Christian belief:

> The Word became flesh and dwelt among us, full of grace and truth; we have beheld his glory, glory as of the only Son from the Father. (John 1:14)

In the unfolding of the lectionary for the season, we see the glory of the only Son. This word *glory* will inform the shaping of the pages to follow. Indeed, the *glory* of God is one of the most frequent motifs in the Scriptures, both Old and New Testaments, appearing in many hundreds of verses. The Psalms are full of God's glory:

> Ascribe to the Lord the *glory* due his name;
>   worship the Lord in the splendor of his holiness.
>   (Psalm 29:2 NIV)

> Not to us, O Lord, not to us,
> but to thy name give *glory*,
>   for the sake of thy steadfast love and thy
>   faithfulness! (Psalm 115:1)

In the biblical languages, the word for glory is *kavod* in Hebrew, *doxa* in Greek. The Greek word *doxa* comes over into English in *doxology*, literally, "to speak glory"—that is, to utter praise to the *doxa* of God. Understanding the glory of Christ requires understanding the importance of *kavod* in the Old Testament. This should be stressed in order to maintain the unity of Jesus Christ with the so-called Old Testament God. They are not two different gods. They are one, and the glory of one is the glory of the other.

"The glory of God" of which we so often hear in the Old Testament does not describe God's essence. A word used to identify that essence is *aseity* (Latin *aseitas*, "being from itself")—God as he is in himself. *Doxa* is one step removed from God's aseity. It is the radiant *revelation of* himself, an emanation of his attributes that humans can receive only by faith. It is his outgoing self-revelation perceived by disciples as dazzling radiance, yes—but more important still, as absolute power.

That is the combination—radiance and power—that makes *glory* one of the most telling words used to describe God in the Bible. Because it denotes God's sheer majesty and dominion, it should always be a companion to attributes like "merciful" and "loving."[2] The glory of the love of Jesus is not the same as human love, because his glory is something that is impossible for unaided humanity: namely, it is able to triumph over all that would destroy it.

The body of Christ needs to recommit to this concept of the glory of God. It has been in semi-eclipse of late, as Jesus has been presented as a moral exemplar, social activist, and religious teacher minus his unique identity as Son of God. Perhaps the very word *glory* seems bombastic to some, for reasons similar to recent attempts at eliminating the idea of Jesus as "Lord." However, the glory of God and the lordship of Christ are too central to the biblical message to be pushed to the side in the church's witness. In particular, the glory of God needs to be recovered as a preaching theme if we are to seek a more obviously revelatory way of proclaiming Christ.[3] The Epiphany season, with its narrative arc shaped by manifestations of Jesus' uniquely divine identity, is well suited to this project.

WHAT *IS* THE GLORY OF GOD?

What resonance does the word *glory* have in today's English language? How often is it used, and with what meaning? The adjective *glorious* is familiar enough—we might say that we saw a "glorious" sunset, and we might hear of a pop star such as Beyoncé "in all her glory." In the Greek and Roman worlds, *glory* was associated with fame, reputation, and, especially, honor. These qualities were to be sought above all else, and most often were particularly associated with military glory. In late antiquity and medieval times, warriors and heroes of song and saga went on long and dangerous journeys to "get glory" for themselves. In the present day as in the ancient world, athletes seek glory in Olympic gold, which is given for crowning achievement. Glory in this sense of renown is for the elite. Usually it is earned, but it can also be bought or stolen. It can be taken away or lost; we often hear of "past glory." It hardly needs to be pointed out that human-based glory is ephemeral. It passes away.

In contrast, the glory ascribed to God throughout the Old Testament is immutable and eternal. Its source is the Creator himself and it emanates from him. It is in the intrinsic character of God to possess this divine radiance. It does not change according to human response or lack thereof. If it is not perceived, it is still there, beyond human power to earn, to give, or to withdraw. At the will of God, it can be withdrawn from humans, but it cannot be withdrawn from the Creator. Therefore it serves as a judgment upon anyone who does not acknowledge it, whether they know it or not.

In the Bible, eternal glory belongs to God alone, and all who are called into service by God know that they can attribute glory only to God. However, we learn from Scripture that in engaging with human beings, God shields his *essence* from us precisely with its *manifestation*; he is willing to shrink himself, so to speak, so that we are not swallowed up alive by his glory. When Moses rather presumptuously asks that God show him his glory, God grants the gift but puts Moses into a cleft of a rock so that he will see only God's back (Exodus 33:18-23).

One of the most memorable biblical visions of God's glory is when God shows himself to the prophet Isaiah in the temple:

Holy, holy, holy, is the Lord of hosts;
the whole earth is full of his glory. (Isaiah 6:3)

Isaiah is completely overcome with fear and trembling. It is important for us to pause over this:

Woe is me! For I am lost; for I am a man of unclean lips, and I dwell in the midst of a people of unclean lips; for my eyes have seen the King, the Lord of hosts! (Isaiah 6:5)

Most of us don't realize what we are singing when we toss off the familiar hymn "Holy, Holy, Holy," or when we sing the *Sanctus* during the eucharistic liturgy. It seems routine to us, but we should notice Isaiah's reaction. His vision of the glory of God results in an instantaneous perception of the *contrast* between God's purity and his people's contamination—their "uncleanness" because of sin. God's glory manifested in the epiphanies of the Bible evoke intense reactions ("The glory of the Lord shone round about them: and they were sore afraid," Luke 2:9-10 KJV). Epiphanies in Scripture are met with reactions of disbelief (Gideon), awe (the Magi), amazement (Cana), or—most often—"fear and trembling." It is precisely for this reason that the biblical angels are always saying "Fear not!"

Perhaps the most seminal of all the manifestations in the Old Testament is that of Moses in the desert and the bush that burns furiously but is not consumed. Moses reacts to the phenomenon as a "great sight," as though it were some sort of magic trick. But God speaks to Moses out of the bush, saying in effect, "Stand back! Do not come near my presence without trembling; take off your shoes; I AM WHO I AM, not who you thought I was."

"And Moses hid his face, for he was afraid to look at God" (Exodus 3:6). We should not come to an epiphany too quickly, before we absorb the message from the burning bush: "Stand back! Too hot to handle!" Exodus continues: "The *appearance of* the *glory* of the Lord was like a devouring fire on the top of the mountain in the sight of the people of Israel" (Exodus 24:17).[4] The glory of God comes upon Moses and Isaiah as a body blow.

The glory of God is not summoned by human striving or wishing. It cannot be conjured up by anything we can do.[5] It is pure gift. It comes to us solely at the will of the Creator. It comes from another dimension, over against the world of human bondage to sin and death. It is not accessible to the unaided human eye. Thus Paul teaches us that "flesh and blood cannot inherit the kingdom of God" (1 Corinthians 15:50), and John says that "no one has ever seen God" directly (John 1:18); in Jesus Christ the living Word, he has been made visible. Only as God chooses do we see God's glory; such a vision is not available as a mere religious option, a human choice among many others. God's glory is not to be confused with sentimental or superficial human ideas of glory. The only entrance into heavenly glory is through God's work and Word in Jesus Christ. If we confuse this with human sight, human potential, human possibility, we have altogether missed the glory of God.

THE UNIQUE GLORY OF GOD IN CHRIST

In dictionaries, definitions of *glory* use words like radiance, splendor, luster, majesty, brilliance, resplendence, grandeur, and effulgence.[6] It is notable that many of these words are associated with light. Jesus Christ himself said, "I am the light of the world" (John 8:12). We are so familiar with this that we don't notice its audacity. Who would talk like this about himself? Yet this is what he says himself in John's Gospel. Wouldn't we think such a person was mentally deranged? How can we defend such statements if Jesus is only one more religious teacher? We need to remember, in proclaiming Jesus, that our gospel makes no earthly sense. The Synoptic Gospels say that when Christ was crucified at noonday, the sun was darkened, because the Light of the World was going out.

Through his life and work Jesus radically altered the definition of *doxa*. The change that comes over the word *doxa* in its journey from secular to biblical Greek is theologically very important. In secular Greek, *doxa* refers to honor given to someone who is thought to have earned it. In New Testament Greek, however, the definition is transformed.[7] In the New Testament as in the Old, only God possesses glory, and the chief vocation of believers is to praise God's glory. This is a significant change in meaning. Human beings actively seek glory, but there is no reason or need for Jesus to "get glory" for himself. Glory has been his since before time began, for it is intrinsically part of his nature as the living three-personed Creator. In his divine nature he does not "need" anything. He purposefully enters into *human* need, experiencing hunger and thirst and weariness like any human being, but his divine being in the Godhead is forever secured. God's *doxa* in Christ is a manifestation of the Old Testament *kabod* carried forward into the new Jerusalem, the abode of God's people in the kingdom to come.

The season of Epiphany offers an opportunity to focus for several weeks on the glory of Christ as the second person of the Trinity, in all his intrinsic, immutable, inestimable glory, which can never pass away. With regard to the glory of God in Jesus Christ, all subjectivity is eliminated. The *doxa* of God is not earned, not negotiable; it is inherent and unchangeable.

The glory of Jesus Christ has some surprising features that could never have been conjured up by human imagination, projection, or wish fulfillment. For example, in the famous prologue of the Fourth Gospel, we are warned that many will not believe:

> The true light that enlightens every man was coming into the world. He was in the world, and the world was made through him, yet the world knew him not. He came to his own home, and his own people received him not. (John 1:9-11)

The promise, however, is made to those who do recognize him:

> But to all who received him, who believed in his name, he gave power to become children of God; who were born, not of blood nor of the will of the flesh nor of the will of man, but of God.
>
> And the Word became flesh and dwelt among us, full of grace and truth; we have beheld his glory, glory as of the only Son from the Father. (John 1:12-14)

John's prologue is always the Gospel reading for Christmas Day. The worshipers are pointed ahead in the direction of the Epiphany season, in which the "glory as of the only Son from the Father" will be displayed. We will learn that many will not receive him, and that his destiny is the opposite of what one would expect from a glorious Messiah (in this way the Gospel reading points ahead to Holy Week). "But to all who receive him," he will bring the uncreated light of God, for he was in the beginning with God, and he was God (John 1:1-2). No definition of glory can be greater than that one. Later in the Fourth Gospel, we see this glory at work in the most extreme circumstances: As Jesus stands with Mary and Martha of Bethany at their brother's tomb, Jesus commands that the very door of death be opened. Martha protests that there will be a stench. Jesus replies, "Did I not tell you that if you would believe you would see the glory of God?" (John 11:39-40).

The apostle Paul demonstrates a proper understanding of God's glory in his vocation as the recipient of the risen Christ's own personal choice. Given his unique stature as apostle to the Gentiles, Paul might have been especially tempted to claim honor for himself, but he did the opposite: he accepted dishonor as part of his job. He looked not for any worldly reward, but for the glory promised to him personally by Christ; the new Christians will be his glory (1 Thessalonians 2:19). Indeed, Paul, having been imprisoned many times and knowing he is likely to be martyred, declares that Christ will be glorified in his own body "whether by life or by death" (Philippians 1:20). Paul's declaration about this is one of those radical statements he makes that cannot be emphasized often enough: the glory of Christ was paradoxically made known in his crucifixion.

> God forbid that I should glory, save in the cross of our Lord Jesus Christ, by whom the world is crucified unto me, and I unto the world. (Galatians 6:14 KJV)

Paul "glories in" the cross, and time-honored hymns contain such lines as, "In the cross of Christ I glory."[8] The sheer audacity of this claim is insufficiently stressed in the preaching and teaching of the church. Throughout the Gospels, we are continually pointed ahead to the shocking culmination of Jesus' earthly ministry. The season of Lent moves toward the scandal of Golgotha as surely as Paul and John the Baptist point to it. The paradox is that Jesus' seeming defeat is actually his glory. John's Gospel specifically refers to the Passion as Jesus' hour of glory (John 12:23; 13:31-32).

The connection between the glory of God shown forth in Christ and the crucifixion of Jesus should never be severed. When the fourth evangelist writes that "we have seen his glory" (John 1:14 NIV), it is not a free-floating attribute; it pertains to him as the Lamb of God who takes away the sin of the world (John 1:29). Paul, the theologian of the cross par excellence, refers constantly to the glory of God in Christ, in one passage writing that "we all, with unveiled face, beholding the *glory* of the Lord, are being changed into his likeness from one degree of *glory* to another" (2 Corinthians 3:18). In this and many other places Paul specifically states that the Christian will partake in this glory: "Through [Christ] we have obtained access to this grace in which we stand, and we rejoice in our hope of sharing the *glory* of God" (Romans 5:2). In one particularly resonant verse Paul states, "Far be it from me to *glory* except in the cross of our Lord Jesus Christ, by which the world has been crucified to me, and I to the world" (Galatians 6:14).

We will return to the cross in the pages to follow, because the Epiphany season leads to it as the very center of the glory of Christ. Indeed, it is precisely as Jesus calls his disciples away from any notion of earthly glory that we see most deeply into what his glory actually is.

EXPRESSING THE INEXPRESSIBLE

The Epiphany season is designed to replace minimalist notions of glory with the real thing. This is a challenging project, because the human psyche is always wired to take credit whenever possible. For example, Wikipedia offers a definition of *glory* as the word "used to describe the manifestation of God's presence *as perceived by* humans according to the Abrahamic religions."[9]

What is wrong with that? If we can answer that question, we will come closer to an understanding of what it is that we learn during Epiphany. Note the subject of the verb in this dictionary definition. It is a word used to describe God's presence "as perceived by humans." God's glory is therefore subjective, not objective. Unless we perceive it, it's not there; it has no use. Its importance depends entirely on our perception. There, in one sentence, we see the difference between "religious" thinking and biblical theology. In most religious (or "spiritual") approaches, our human capacities are at the forefront.

Contrarily, in biblical theology God is the subject of the sentences about himself. He is not an object of our perception. He *originates* our perception, *guides* our perception, *corrects* our perception. Think of Job when he has actually been confronted with God himself, at God's own instigation: "I [have] uttered that I understood not; things too wonderful for me, which I knew not. . . . I have heard of thee by the hearing of the ear: but now mine eye seeth thee. . . . I abhor myself, and repent in dust and ashes" (Job 42:3-6 KJV).

We could use a lot more of this "shock and awe" in our teaching about the glory of God. Isaiah, for instance, minces no words:

> Enter into the rock,
>   and hide in the dust
> from before the terror of the Lord,
>   and from the glory of his majesty. (Isaiah 2:10)

Scripture makes it clear that we cannot look at God's glory directly. It has to be mediated to us, as this hymn affirms:

> Great Father of glory, pure Father of light,
> Thine angels adore thee, all veiling their sight;

All laud we would render, O help us to see
'tis only the splendor of light hideth thee.[10]

Actually describing the glory of God is, in a sense, an impossible task. It requires indirection, as in the phrase "as it were." The prophet Ezekiel has demonstrated this in one of the most mesmerizing, mysterious images in the entire Scripture. His book begins this way:

> The word of the Lord came to Ezekiel the priest . . .
> in the land of the Chaldeans by the river Chebar;
> and the hand of the Lord was upon him there.
> (Ezekiel 1:3)[11]

Then Ezekiel speaks:

> As I looked, behold, a stormy wind came out of the north, and a great cloud, with brightness round about it, and fire flashing forth continually, and in the midst of the fire, *as it were* gleaming bronze. (Ezekiel 1:4)

This is developed for eleven verses, and then comes the famous vision of the wheels within wheels:

> As for the appearance of the wheels and their construction: their appearance *was like* the gleaming of

a chrysolite; and the four had the same likeness,
their construction being *as it were* a wheel within a
wheel. (Ezekiel 1:16)

This goes on for several more verses, and then the key to
it all:

Such was the *appearance of* the *likeness of* the *glory of*
the Lord. And when I saw it, I fell upon my face, and
I heard the voice of one speaking. (Ezekiel 1:28)[12]

The glory of the Lord is described here with extreme
awe. This is shown in the way the description of the sur-
passingly strange vision is distanced three times from the
perception of the prophet. Note the three *of*s, meant to
emphasize the impossibility of actually describing or ap-
proaching God via human perception.[13] Clearly the
passage is meant to express the inexpressible, something
arriving from another sphere inaccessible to our human
faculties. Nothing is said of Ezekiel's "spiritual preparation" for receiving this epiphany; it arrives independent
of human effort, according to God's own volition.

There are a great many passages in the Scriptures that
refer to the transcendent nature of the glory of God and
its unlikeness to anything comparable on earth. Paul

struggles to express God's glory (some would say only partially successfully!):

> There are celestial bodies and there are terrestrial bodies; but the glory of the celestial is one, and the glory of the terrestrial is another. There is one glory of the sun, and another glory of the moon, and another glory of the stars; for star differs from star in glory.
>
> So it is with the resurrection of the dead. What is sown is perishable, what is raised is imperishable. It is sown in dishonor, it is raised in glory. (1 Corinthians 15:40-42)

Paul gives up his attempts to create analogies:

> I tell you this, brethren: flesh and blood cannot inherit the kingdom of God, nor does the perishable inherit the imperishable. (1 Corinthians 15:50)

Paul finishes his extraordinary exposition with the words, "we shall be changed" (1 Corinthians 15:52).[14] He speaks of the resurrection to eternal life, but even in our present life, the power of this hope of transformation is the moving force in the church's worship as we acknowledge the risen and reigning Lord by giving ultimate glory to him.

The biblical testimony to the glory of God is always to be understood as God's choice. Karl Barth bases his entire massive theological project on the conviction that knowledge of God is "grounded entirely in the miracle of grace."[15] Clearly the vision of Ezekiel was vouchsafed, not earned. The season of Epiphany is designed to show that there is no road to the glory of God through human seeking; it cannot be summoned by human endeavor. It cannot be repeated too often: it comes as pure gift. It is revealed only from God's being, from his will and his self-revelation, for the salvation of his creatures.

There was a time when Episcopal clergy memorized and often used this ascription from the epistle to Jude:

Now to him who is able to keep you from falling and to present you without blemish before *the presence of his glory* with rejoicing, to the only God, our Savior through Jesus Christ our Lord, *be glory, majesty, dominion, and authority*, before all time and now and for ever. Amen. (Jude 24-25)

These two verses of Scripture say a good deal about the glory of God that we emphasize during Epiphany:

- God *is able* to save us not only in the present but also in his eternal future.[16]

- Through his Son our Lord Jesus Christ, he is our only God and Savior.

- God is eternally himself, in glory, from before time and beyond time.

THE GLORIFICATION OF GOD AS ENJOYMENT

The first sequence in the Westminster Shorter Catechism is time-tested and much loved by many:

Q. 1. What is the chief end of man?[17]
A. Man's chief end is to glorify God, and to enjoy him for ever.[18]

We may not like the use of the generic word *man*, but if we try to update this, we would also have to lose the word *enjoy*, because it is very unlikely that anyone today would use it in this ever-so-slightly-bygone way. We might have chosen *delight in*. In any case, the calling of human beings to glorify God is affirmed as though it were the same thing as "enjoying" God—relishing, savoring, delighting in his presence. Our common, colloquial use of *enjoy* without an object is indeed a poor thing compared to the "enjoyment" of the glory of God. To enjoy a meal, or a movie, or an evening out is to take fleeting pleasure in a brief and perishing moment. The summons of the Scripture is a summons to a life of purified and everlasting joy, not in some fleeting hour or destructible object, but as our eternal future in the age to come, where we—in the fellowship of all the redeemed—are to become purified recipients of the love of God. Enjoying God means to "glorify" God and to take delight in doing so. The Epiphany season is designed to teach us to glorify Jesus Christ and to "enjoy" his presence in this way. It is a strange glory, because it points to the cross, but it is a glory just the same—infinitely more than any glory that the world can offer or even imagine.

Precursors of this joy are available to us even now in the worship of the people of God, as we are lifted out of ourselves to behold his excellence and majesty—for the glory of the Lord Christ is far more than his own radiance and majesty. His glory is not simply an attribute that causes awe and wonder in the worshiper. Crucially, it is also his to give. The Heidelberg Catechism, much loved for its pastoral warmth, affirms: "Because I belong to him, Christ, by his Holy Spirit, assures me of eternal life and makes me wholeheartedly willing and ready from now on to live for him." This is the glory of life in Christ. Such a life is secure in the purpose of God.

But, we might protest, we are not living wholeheartedly in this way. We are anything but wholehearted. What then? To which the answer is always, "I belong to him." That is *our* glory, as given by him to us. And he gives it along with his power, power to defend us from our own sinful condition and "keep us safe from all enemies." This is unconditional, you'll notice. But there is more. The unconditional gift of the glory of Christ our head is defined by his gifts—gifts of "true righteousness and holiness" that take root and grow in us. Such gifts keep us safe precisely because this power is his to give.

In one of his most original and revelatory sermon-essays, "The Weight of Glory," C. S. Lewis opens up an unexpected aspect of the glory of God. God's "brightness, splendour, luminosity" is not only something intrinsic to God, but is also something God promises to give to all who love him. Lewis then goes on to affirm that we do not simply observe the glory of God from outside but are actually taken into it according to his promise: "We are to shine as the sun, we are to be given the Morning Star."[19]

This is an eschatological gift, bestowed from the future, belonging to God's redeemed creation yet to come.[20] This is the deep meaning of the phrase "changed from glory into glory, till in heaven we take our place."[21] Even now, as we ponder the glory of God, we can begin to understand how he promises to work in us toward our perfection, through "the glories of his righteousness and wonders of his love."[22] We can even speak of God's glory being our own:

> Thou, O Lord, art a shield about me,
>   my *glory*, and the lifter of my head. (Psalm 3:3)

Thus the incomparable George Herbert writes of our glorification in his poem "The Star":

> Bright spark, shot from a brighter place,
>   Where beams surround my Saviour's face,
>   Canst thou be any where
>   So well as there?
> Yet if thou wilt from thence depart,
>   Take a bad lodging in my heart. . . .

First with thy fire-work burn to dust
    Folly, and worse than folly, lust:
        Then with thy light refine,
           And make it shine.
So disengaged from sin and sickness,
    Touch it with thy celestial quickness,
        That it may hang and move
           After thy love.[23]

Herbert, with his special gift of addressing the individual conscience, shows how the radiance of God is not something simply to wonder at, but so much more: it is the promised gift of a "refined" and transformed human heart both now and in the kingdom yet to come. Joy is bestowed upon us through the transformative power of God's glory. This is the deepest meaning of the phrase "from glory into glory." A resounding baptismal declaration of the early church announces, "He has delivered us from the dominion of darkness and transferred us to the kingdom of his beloved Son" (Colossians 1:13). Because this deliverance is of God, it has—as it were— already occurred; it is an eschatological event planted in the present.

This special emphasis of Epiphany is needed by the church right now as a drowning person needs a lifeboat. Paul identifies it in one of his letters to his most troublesome church, the one in Corinth. He is greatly distressed by its members turning away from the true gospel to false preachers who are teaching a distorted message. They have even resorted to personal attacks on him in order to win over the congregation. He writes an impassioned letter to his people in Corinth, fearing to lose them.[24] Here is a sample of what he wrote; there is no passage in all of Scripture more apt for teaching in Epiphany than this one:

> Unbelievers [do not see] the light of the gospel of the *glory* of Christ, *who is the likeness of God.* For what we preach is not ourselves, but Jesus Christ as Lord, with ourselves as your servants for Jesus' sake. For it is the God who said, "Let light shine out of darkness," who has shone in our hearts to give the light of the knowledge of the *glory* of God in the face of Christ. (2 Corinthians 4:4-6)

This is as close as we are going to be able to come to understanding what the season of Epiphany is designed to be and to teach. From its beginning by the light of a star to its culmination on the mountain of transfiguration, its Sundays are designed to display *the glory of Christ who is the likeness of God*, shining in and transforming our hearts even now. As the Epiphany hymn quoted earlier puts it, the season teaches "God in flesh made manifest." What we preach is Jesus Christ as Lord over every hostile power that would enslave his creation. As the church—the bride of Christ—recommits herself to the praise of his glory, he himself accompanies the promises of his Word through his living and powerful presence in its worship, in its fellowship, and in its self-giving service. In the praises of the church, the Lord lives:

> All *glory* be to God on high,
> and peace on earth from heaven,
> and God's good will unfailingly
> be to all people given.
> We bless, we worship you, we raise
> for your *great glory* thanks and praise,
> O God almighty Father.
>
> O Lamb of God, Lord Jesus Christ,
> whom God the Father gave us,

who for the world was sacrificed
upon the cross to save us;
and as you sit on God's right hand
and we for judgment there must stand,
Have mercy, Lord, upon us.

You only are the Holy One,
who came for our salvation,
And only you are God's true Son,
who was before creation.
You only, Christ, as Lord we own
and *with the Spirit, you alone
share in the Father's glory.*[25]

2

The Day

The history of the church in the first three centuries after Christ is not always as straightforward as we might wish. We would like to know more about the shaping of the liturgical calendar during those centuries. However that may be, January 6 is as firmly lodged in the calendar for the Feast of the Epiphany as any Christian holy day has ever been. It is well attested that this date for Epiphany was solidly established in the Eastern church from the third century AD forward, and in the West, a Roman source in AD 361 referred to January 6 as the fixed date for observing the Epiphany.[1] Thus the celebration of Epiphany on an assigned date, January 6, significantly preceded that of Christmas Day. Indeed, and remarkably, it ranked with Easter and Pentecost as one of the three principal festival days of the church.[2]

We need not give further attention to the origins of the feast day except to stress its ancient character. More important is the nature of the observance itself. The early celebration of Epiphany should teach us something about its neglect in the present culture, with our perhaps excessive emphasis on Christmas. Christmas observance in our own time—at least since the Victorian age—is almost entirely held captive to the manger story, illustrated by a crèche displaying an infant in a stable with animals, generally restricted to the theme of nativity. However, for observant worshipers in liturgical churches, the irreducible emphasis on Christmas as the Feast of the Incarnation is secured even today by the traditional reading for Christmas Day, the Prologue of John's Gospel ("In the beginning was the Word . . . and the Word was God"). This passage links the Feast of the Nativity with the revelation of Christ to the Gentiles represented by the Magi; the Prologue can therefore serve to point our attention ahead to what will become the fullest significance of the Epiphany season:

> We have beheld his glory, glory as of the only Son from the Father. (John 1:14)

This heightened attention to theological significance seems to have been attractive to the Eastern Church, for it adopted the story of the baptism of Jesus by John the Baptist in the Jordan River as the central motif of the Epiphany festival on January 6. Let's recall that *epiphaneia* means "manifestation," and it follows that baptism was the first occasion for the *manifestation* of the adult Jesus as Son of God (Matthew 3:16-17 and parallels). To this day, the Eastern churches celebrate not the gifts of the Magi but the water of baptism as the central symbolism of January 6, and the ceremony of the blessing of the waters is part of the day's rituals.[3] The liturgical churches of the West have hurried to catch up in recent decades, with heightened interest in the baptism on the first Sunday after the Epiphany. The older Book of Common Prayer of the Episcopal Church placed the story of the baptism on the second Sunday after the Epiphany; the 1989 Book of Common Prayer has helpfully moved it to the *first* Sunday, thus honoring its importance in the ancient church and, even more significantly, in the life of the church in every age of the world. In other liturgical denominations, notably the Lutheran, baptism remains central to the Christian story and Christian identity. It is therefore highly recommended that baptisms be scheduled for the first Sunday after the Epiphany. (We will discuss this further in chapter five.)

CELEBRATING THE FEAST ON JANUARY 6

The challenge for the churches in our time is to find a proper way of celebrating this important feast day, since it turns up on a Sunday only once every seven years, and it is often difficult, given the way people live today, to attract people to come to a service in midweek. This is especially challenging for the Feast of Epiphany, because it is too important to be treated in a perfunctory way.

There are several ways to attract a good attendance at an Epiphany liturgy on a weekday evening. First and most important is to guarantee that the service is very well done, befitting the importance of the day, with much thought given to it and with attention to details, like having an attractive printed order of service. The hymns should be carefully chosen—in addition to the well-known "We Three Kings of Orient Are" there are several excellent ones in the Episcopal and Lutheran hymnals (note especially "Songs of thankfulness and praise" with its emphasis on manifestation). The proper antiphons and prayers should be used (every local congregation should have readily accessible copies of traditional liturgical resources). On the days preceding the Epiphany, the congregation can be instructed about the ancient origins of the festival and its great theological significance. Ideally it would be on the day itself, January 6. Any departure from this loses its connection to the wisdom of the early church.

In addition to these deeply rooted ways of encouraging people to take Epiphany with the seriousness it deserves, there are some time-honored strategies for guaranteed attendance. One is always to involve children. Have an Epiphany procession. Get them dressed up as wise men and camel drivers in exotic costumes and they will come—and so will their parents. Even more edifying is to have a children and youth choir, which will not only attract extended families to come to hear their children sing, but will also give the youngsters some background in sacred music. Another guaranteed (and biblical) enticement is to have a festive meal after the service (with exploding "crackers" for the children, perhaps?). Potlucks can be very popular. This is a tried-and-true strategy to keep people coming to church, and one should not be shy about using it.

Finally, the sermon for the Feast of the Epiphany should strive to teach something of the deep meaning of this holy day when Jesus Christ is manifested to those who have been outside the boundaries of the promises of God. The second chapter of the letter to the Ephesians beautifully expounds this. In Christ, God has "broken down the dividing wall of hostility" (Ephesians 2:14) between the people of God and those who are "strangers to the covenants of promise . . . and without God in the world" (Ephesians 2:12), for Christ has reconciled us "both to God in one body through the cross" (Ephesians 2:16). This, truly, is his glory—and in this era when racial and ethnic separation and hostility seem to be at a boiling point around the world, it is more central to the gospel proclamation than ever.

3

The Season

In his book *Celebrating Liturgical Time*, Neil Alexander declares forthrightly, "The Feast of the Epiphany is older than the Feast of Christmas and possesses a much richer tapestry of themes."[1] We have already begun to illustrate this tapestry. The ancient feast on January 6 is followed by "the season after the Epiphany" as we still have it today.[2] It is designed as a narrative that displays an arc of God's revelation, beginning in the infancy of Jesus and moving quickly into his entrance upon his public ministry at his baptism, followed by examples of his miracles, healings, and teaching, reaching a climax in the transfiguration—the *epiphaneia* at Mount Tabor—the crowning event of the Epiphany season before the beginning of Lent. If preachers follow this ancient and hallowed plot, either with passages from the lectionary or with other passages that focus on other manifestations of

Jesus' divine origin and identity, the congregation will develop a heightened sense of Holy Week and the depths to which our God is prepared to descend in order to bring us into his eternal glory.

The liturgical calendar as we know it today goes back to the earliest centuries after Christ, but it was not formed overnight. The development of the interrelated festivals of Christmas and Epiphany is particularly convoluted, subject to heated debate, and as such best left to scholars.[3] A brief sketch, however, will interest anyone who cares about Christian worship.

What is known for certain is that by the fifth century AD four themes for the Epiphany had become firmly fixed in the greater part of Christendom:

1. The visit of the Magi

2. The baptism in the Jordan River

3. The miracle of the wine at the wedding at Cana

4. The transfiguration of Christ in the presence of his chosen disciples.

The first three signs, the *tria miracula*, were well-established in Gaul by the fifth century. The fourth, the transfiguration on the mountain (*transformationis in monte*), was attached to the season at relatively the same time in the church in northern Italy.[4] It is remarkable that these four biblical motifs were so thoroughly fixed to Epiphany in the earliest centuries that we can participate in the sacred biblical scenes in essentially the same way today, reading and reflecting upon each of them as manifestations of Jesus' identity. That identity, revealed in the testimony of the apostles and evangelists, was theologically expounded in the councils of the early church, in what must be counted as one of the greatest feats of intellectual achievement in human history. Christians can be justifiably proud of the work of Athanasius, the three Cappadocian fathers, Hilary of Poitiers, and others for giving us an aesthetically beautiful and intellectually satisfying body of work leading us to a robust confession of Jesus Christ, "of one substance with the Father," and of the Trinity of persons. This is one of the features of the Epiphany season. If we are looking for it, we can see as the patristic scholars did—an orthodox Christology taking shape Sunday by Sunday. We should not be afraid of a few big words. If people can understand what *theology* is (*theos*/God, *logos*/Word—the doctrine of God), they can understand what *Christology* is (Christ-word—the doctrine of how Jesus is Son of God). Our churches have been sorely lacking in such teaching in a time when the renewal of the church depends on it. The Epiphany season gives us an unexcelled opportunity to proclaim a powerful, confident Christology grounded in the testimonies of the apostolic witnesses who were ready to die for their Lord.

As we've seen in the previous chapter, Epiphany itself is a specific feast day, not a whole season. The Sundays following January 6 are not "*of* Epiphany," but "*after* [the] Epiphany."[5] The lectionary now in wide use in many English-speaking churches is remarkably faithful in combining the ancient biblical motifs in a narrative sequence, carrying the people of God through a series of episodes that show forth the identity, mission, destiny, and glory of Christ. In fact, when the readings are taken with those of Advent and Lent, the narrative thrust of Epiphany is particularly . . . well, *revelatory*. It should therefore be prized for its own sake as a rich collection of the biblical sources for maximum effect in the liturgical year.[6] If preachers and teachers follow this plot, the congregation will develop a heightened sense of the incongruity between *glory* and *crucifixion*, which marks the Christian gospel as unique in the world of religion.

The central question about the identity of Jesus can be framed in several ways. For instance, Matthew's Gospel poses the question as Jesus' own, from the last week of his life as he confronted his enemies:

> While the Pharisees were gathered together, Jesus asked them, Saying, What think ye of Christ? whose son is he? (Matthew 22:41-42 KJV)

This question, "What think ye of Christ?" (especially in its King James translation), has had a rich history in the evangelistic preaching of the church.[7] Another equally challenging question is posed by Jesus in the episode called the Confession of Peter, which appears in all three Synoptics (Matthew 16:15-16; Mark 8:29-30; Luke 9:20). "Who do you say that I am?" Never mind about who John the Baptist and the other prophets are, Jesus is telling the disciples—it's me that you must fasten your eyes upon. And never mind what others say about me. They don't know me. Who do *you* say that I am? The season after the Epiphany is the time for reflecting upon that question for ourselves . . . the question posed by the Savior himself.

4

The Star

The famous story of the three wise men, or sages—alternatively Magi (Greek *magoi*)—is the centerpiece of the Feast of the Epiphany on January 6.[1] The passage from Matthew is always read on this day.

Only Matthew tells of the Magi; the shepherds and the angel are only in Luke. It is remarkable that Matthew focuses exclusively on these unusual visitors when describing the events of Jesus' birth and infancy. He and Luke are telling us quite different (though complementary) things, and it is helpful for us to consider why Matthew has made the visit of the Magi his central focus.

To begin with, it must be admitted that we do not know much about these mysterious visitors. Exceptional economy in storytelling is typical of the biblical writers; Matthew is reticent where later tradition has been extravagant. We have no idea how many Magi there were,

let alone their names, races, or characteristics. Extra-
biblical legend has supplied the number three, probably
based on Matthew's statement that there were three gifts.
Out of his unadorned story a host of supplemental details has grown, including names for three *magoi* and a
different ethnic identity for each, and the day has traditionally been an opportunity for a lavishly costumed
procession in regal costumes.[2] Artists have always de-
lighted in depicting the three visitors with their richly
caparisoned camels and splendidly appareled retinue.
The most far-fetched outcome has been the claim, per-
sisting to this day, that their bones repose in Cologne
Cathedral in Germany.

On the feast day of the Epiphany, Evelyn Waugh—a
devout Catholic—wrote in his journal that Epiphany is
preeminently the feast of artists. Well, no (although it
would be churlish to deprive the tradition of its inherited
richness). It is important to get past this quest for orna-
mentation that is of no interest to the evangelist.
Matthew was not writing for the lavish imaginations of
painters of pictures, makers of costumes, or directors of
pageants.[3] He did not have pilgrimages to shrines or reli-
quaries in mind. He was writing for his own Christian

community, a community in urgent need of guidance about crucial questions.

In Matthew's time, toward the end of the first century, it was becoming clear that most Jews were not becoming Christ-followers (indeed, this was already apparent in Paul's day—see Romans 9–11).[4] This perceived crisis raised many disturbing questions. Did this mean that all the prophecies concerning Israel had failed? And even more immediately, what was the relationship of the Gentiles to the King of the Jews? And why were the Pharisees in the Synagogue persecuting Christians at this time?[5] In the latter part of the first century, a time of increased tension between the infant church and the ancient synagogue, Matthew reached back into his rich sources of information about Jesus and produced the story that no other evangelist had told. Matthew has nothing to say about lambs, donkeys, or stables. Everything he wants us to know about the infancy of Jesus is in the story of the Magi. If we are attentive, it tells us much of what we need to know about the relation of Jews and Gentiles in the light of the star.

Again, we should make an effort to strip away all the accumulated accretions. Matthew's story is bare of detail.

The chief personages (their number is not mentioned) are identified simply as *magoi*—sages, or wise men. (In our present era, they are often called "astrologers," but this is misleading: insofar as they consulted the stars, it would have been an aspect of ancient learning, not of fortune-telling.) They are "from the East," a phrase which is suitably vague; it is most commonly thought to be Persia, Babylon, or Arabia. The most important factor is that *they are Gentiles.* They are not part of the previously elect people of God. In the persons of the Magi, Matthew "is anticipating the Gentile Christians in his own community."[6] By the time Matthew wrote, the predominance of Gentiles in the church was clearly an issue to be faced. Here is the center of the significance of the exotic strangers who appear in the midst of Jewry.

It is striking that when they arrive in Jerusalem, they ask people whom they meet, "Where is he who has been born King of the Jews?" It is clear that Herod, the local representative of the Roman Empire, is existentially threatened by this.[7] He "summons them secretly" to find out what they know about this rival. In this way, Matthew's narrative makes the claim that Jesus, the living Lord who is gathering the Gentiles into his community, was born the King of the Jews and remains the King of the Jews. His identity as the one foreseen by the Hebrew prophets is secured; if there were to be any doubt about that, Matthew seals it soon hereafter with the story of the Presentation in the temple (which we will shortly describe).

King Herod, therefore, is not the King of the Jews, but a usurper. This is something that Herod fears, even though he does not know his own Scriptures and must call in the chief priests and scribes to explain them; thus he contrives to learn the location of this infant King of the Jews so that he can do away with him. When the holy family escapes him, guided by God's angel sent for the purpose, he flies into a murderous rage and kills all the male Hebrew babies in Bethlehem that his soldiers can find.

Presentations of the Matthean narrative that have had such an illustrious life in art and imagination are not complete without the disturbing involvement of Herod and the political killings that result from the Magi's visit. This was a truth acknowledged by the ancient church when it placed a Holy Innocents Day in the week after Christmas Day. If the church really wanted to honor the Magi, we would have Epiphany pageants that tell the whole

Matthean story, including this dark aspect that is indispensable to Matthew's intent.

We have at least one surviving Christmas carol from a mystery play of the Middle Ages:

> Herod the king, in his raging,
> Chargèd he hath this day
> His men of might in his own sight
> All young children to slay.[8]

The medieval mind was not as sentimental as ours. The Coventry play, unlike our "Christmas" pageants, did not skim past the dark events that followed upon the visit of the Magi. We can't confirm the mass murder of babies in the historical record, but it is a fact that Herod the Great who ruled Israel at this time was a brute. The story of the Slaughter of the Innocents, as the church calls it, is commensurate with his nature. This is a reminder that the birth of the baby Jesus was not simply a sweet occasion to be memorialized in peaceful nativity scenes. When Matthew compares the massacre to Jeremiah's prophecy about "Rachel weeping for her children" (see Jeremiah 31:15), he is telling us that the Slaughter of the Innocents is symptomatic of the operations of the primeval adversary whose temptations Jesus will resist for forty days in the wilderness two chapters later. Matthew wants us to understand that the advent of the infant King of the Jews is marked by peril and suffering. The holy child is faced with danger at the time of his birth, being driven with his parents as refugees into exile in Egypt for several years; thus the Son of God was a participant in human distress from the beginning.[9]

Again, Matthew helps us to see that this infant King of the Jews will immediately meet with direct opposition from the great adversary of God. Satan and his legions occupied this planet as a result of the fall of humankind, holding the creation and all its creatures in the grip of sin and death (Genesis 1–3; Romans 7:8-11). Jesus was born precisely to engage in a battle to the death with this enemy who will stoop to anything whatsoever to maintain his sovereignty: "This little babe, not three days old, is come to rifle Satan's fold . . . *Deo gracias*."[10] Matthew means to show that the only possible victory over this malevolent force is in the coming of the King himself, the true ruler not only of the Jews but also equally of the Gentiles. He remains the King of the Jews; he also becomes the Lord of the Gentiles. Thus we read the indispensable passage from Ephesians:

Therefore remember that at one time you Gentiles in the flesh . . . were at that time separated from Christ, alienated from the commonwealth of Israel, and strangers to the covenants of promise, having no hope and without God in the world. But now in Christ Jesus you who once were far off have been brought near in the blood of Christ. For he is our peace, who has made us both one. (Ephesians 2:11-14)

The manner in which Matthew tells of the meeting of the Magi with Herod puts into place a Christology of lordship. The strangers seem to understand that Herod is of no importance to them as far as universal rule is concerned; they seek a greater ruler. This is where Jesus' kingship ("born a child and yet a King"[11]) is manifested. The fact that they "return home another way" is not only because they are warned; Matthew's concise conclusion at this point indicates that Herod is an indifferent factor in their long journey. It is a journey directed from beginning to end by the unseen but ever-present God. Herod's puffed-up self-importance evaporates in comparison to the one they have found and worshiped. In the English language, *worship* is an important word. It comes from ancient Anglo-Saxon and means "worth-ship"—to ascribe *ultimate worth* to something or someone. Matthew is portraying the nature of the newborn Jesus in ultimate terms, meaning that there is no one else worthy of worship except him. The fact that he is an utterly helpless, dependent infant heightens the contrast between all worldly power and pomp compared to the glory that is revealed to them by the guidance of the star.

The meaning of the star will never be further illuminated by astronomical inquiries, even in this era of advanced scientific inquiry. The star is not meant to be literally understood as an event in the Kuiper Belt or any other extraterrestrial phenomenon. We interpret it theologically in its scriptural context, as one of the heavenly bodies that are commanded by their Creator:

> Lift up your eyes on high and see:
>   who created these?
> He who brings out their host by number,
>   calling them all by name. (Isaiah 40:26)

That is a thrilling passage when it is placed alongside the story of the Magi, and expands it beyond what it directly says. It is the Creator himself who has commanded a star to lead the Gentile world to the King of the Jews.

The reconciliation of Jews and Gentiles is part of the deep narrative of the foreign visitors to the throne of Israel. On the most profound level, Jesus himself, as the Jewish Messiah, is the eschatological occupant of the throne (Revelation 7:17) in the kingdom to come where that reconciliation will be fully accomplished forever.

A later passage in Isaiah is even more surely related to the Matthean story. Subsequent generations have mined that chapter for interpreting Matthew, and that in itself would account for all the splendor that has attached itself to the idea of the Gentiles coming to the light as kings, mounted upon camels, bearing "the wealth of nations," all of it symbolizing the lordship of the one God over all of the peoples of the earth and all of their accumulated riches:

> Arise, shine; for your light has come,
>> and *the glory of the Lord* has risen upon you. . . .
> And nations shall come to your light,
>> and kings to the brightness of your rising. . . .
>> the wealth of the nations shall come to you.
> A multitude of camels shall cover you,
>> the young camels of Mid'ian and Ephah;
>> all those from Sheba shall come.

They shall bring gold and frankincense,
   and shall proclaim the praise of the Lord.
      (Isaiah 60:1-6)

The arrival of the Gentiles with rich gifts led by a star
brings Revelation 21 to mind as well:

> The city [of God] has no need of sun or moon to
> shine upon it, for the glory of God is its light, and its
> lamp is the Lamb. By its light will the nations walk;
> and the kings of the earth shall bring their glory into
> it, . . . they shall bring into it the glory and the honor
> of the nations. (Revelation 21:23-26)

In the accumulated tradition that transformed the
Magi into kings, the passages from Isaiah and Revelation
stretch the interpretation to include "the [Gentile] nations" who, redeemed from idolatry, will present their
purified treasures. That redemption will be their glory, reflected in the light of the Lamb of God. The final incoming
of the Gentiles will be the climactic eschatological sign
that all is finished: *consummatum est.*[12]

THE FEAST OF THE PRESENTATION OF THE LORD AT THE TEMPLE (CANDLEMAS)

As we've noted, Luke does not tell the story of the adoration of the Magi. Instead, Luke narrates another distinctive occasion within the Epiphany season that teaches the same theme. The two pious parents (Joseph is honored here by being called Jesus' father) bring their forty-day-old infant to the temple to be presented to the High Priest as Jewish law requires (Leviticus 12:1-8). What happened there has been incorporated into the night prayers of the church since at least the fifth century—almost certainly longer—in the form of the canticle (song) of Simeon, traditionally called the *Nunc Dimittis* ("now let depart").[13] The aged Simeon takes up the baby and, holding him in his arms, utters these hallowed words:

> Lord, now lettest thou thy servant depart in peace,
> according to thy word:
> for mine eyes have seen thy salvation,
> which thou hast prepared before the face of
>   all people;
> *a light to lighten the Gentiles,*
> *And to be the glory of thy people Israel.* (1928 Book
>   of Common Prayer version of Luke 2:29-32)

Thus, the significance of the Presentation is linked from one evangelist's story to another. In Luke, the infant Messiah is an epiphany of God's salvation as "a light to lighten the Gentiles." In Matthew's story of the Magi, the star is the cosmic sign that God uses to draw to himself those who are "strangers to the covenants of promise"— that is, all non-Jews everywhere in the world (Ephesians 2:12). The Gentiles, represented by the scholarly Magi, are drawn to worship the God who is the Author of all wisdom and all knowledge. He is King of all kings, Lord of all lords (specifically including the alarmed Herod Antipas). He is the One to whom all homage is paid, all worship is due. Simeon's canticle (a poem suitable for singing) stands alongside the Magi story, for Luke identifies the Presentation even more specifically as a *double epiphany*: the manifestation of the infant as both the glory of Israel *and* the Light of the Gentiles. At the same time, Simeon's enraptured testimony dramatizes the link to the promises given specifically to the Jews, for the Presentation story, like all of the first two chapters of Luke, is steeped in Hebraic atmosphere, particularly that of the temple.[14]

In the Eastern church the feast day is called the Meeting of the Lord (with the aged prophets Simeon and Anna) and has been observed since at least the fourth century. In the West, the full official title is The Presentation of Our Lord Jesus Christ in the Temple. The informal name for the liturgy of the Presentation in the Anglophone world is Candlemas because it features the procession of candles into the church as the antiphon *Lumen ad revelationem* (light of revelation) is chanted. This often overlooked and underappreciated feast of the Lord is always on February 2. The importance and attraction of weekday services on proper days has already been discussed in the chapter two. The church is strengthened by liturgical observance calling for worship at punctuation points on the calendar no matter when they occur during the secular workweek. The Presentation is not a minor occasion: it is certainly one of the epiphanies in which God acts to reveal his Son as the Savior of the whole world. Simeon and Anna, the chief characters in the story, come and go quickly in the Gospel of Luke, but their devotion is a precious treasure that the church has never forgotten, and their extreme age, together with their decades of faithful presence and their prophetic utterances, establishes them as prophets and elders worthy of honor in the story of the church two thousand years later.

The Epiphany season is a radiant time in the church year, but the New Testament always gives us hints of what is to come. Immediately following his testimony to Jesus' identity and his valediction, Simeon has something more disturbing to say. He speaks to Mary:

> Behold, this child is set for the fall and rising of
>   many in Israel,
> and for a sign that is spoken against
> (and a sword will pierce through your own soul
>   also). (Luke 2:34-35)

And so, even in the breathtaking moment of revelation, the shadow of Jesus' Passion and crucifixion is already present. This infant will become a man who will be "spoken against" not only by Jewish and Gentile rulers alike, but even by his own disciples. He will give himself up for torture and a miserable death on a cross, abandoned by those he came to deliver. This is the preordained climax toward which all the various *epiphanies* move.

5

The River

It is widely accepted that the baptism of Jesus in the River Jordan is a central motif of what used to be called the Epiphany Octave—the eight days including January 6 and the following Sunday. Liturgical churches in the West as well as the East have maintained this ancient emphasis, and so the first Sunday after the Epiphany is a particularly suitable time to schedule baptisms of new Christians.

As far back as we can trace the observances of the Eastern Church, a chief feature of the liturgy of the day was the ritual of the sanctification of water—baptismal water in particular, but by extension the sanctification of all the waters of the earth.[1] In Western churches, however, the blessing of water, while it may be included, was (and is) a minor feature. As we shall see, the liturgical shaping of the various Sundays after Epiphany make clear that the theme of the season—whether West or East—continues to be the manifestation of the glory of Christ.

The inaugural event of Jesus' public ministry was his coming to John for baptism. The drama and magnitude of this occasion is not always sufficiently emphasized. Prior to this event, Jesus' special status was known only to a tiny few: his mother (and Joseph perhaps), a handful of shepherds, a small group of Gentile stargazers, two elderly Jews in the temple at Jerusalem, and an assortment of Hebrew scholars twelve years later, who were astonished by his mastery of the Scriptures and his personal charisma. Except for that one brief glimpse of the preternaturally wise young Jesus, the New Testament allows no speculation whatsoever about the childhood and adolescence of Jesus of Nazareth. It is therefore an exceptionally dramatic and significant tableau when he takes his first fateful steps from obscure anonymity onto a large and very crowded stage. He appears alone and unheralded at the waterside where John the Baptist, a true celebrity of his time, was attracting energized multitudes.

We can only wonder at what must have been the inner workings of Jesus' mind as he wrestled with his identity during his formative years. We see him on the bank of the

River Jordan as if for the first time. His quiet, unannounced way of presenting himself heightens the effect. This is the moment awaited by Israel—the arrival of the Messiah. If we pause over this, we will recognize what a momentous occasion it is on a number of levels.

Following the baptism, there must have been a good deal of buzz about this mysterious young man who causes the rock-star prophet to fall back on his heels—and then immediately disappears into the desert for forty days.[2] However, Jesus will soon enough embark on his public ministry. This ministry will consist not just of teachings, but also of public displays of authority. Many people, Christians and non-Christians alike, speak of Jesus in terms almost exclusively of his teaching, but the season following the Feast of the Epiphany has been designed from the beginning to manifest his commanding identity, not only as a charismatic teacher, but also as the definitive, living manifestation of the long-expected Messiah of Israel. On the occasion of his baptism the voice of God speaks: "This is my beloved Son," and on the Mount of Transfiguration at the end of the season, the voice comes again: "This is my beloved Son; listen to him." We may doubt whether the voice was heard by the general public at the river, and on the mountain only three of the disciples heard God speak. These two narratives are therefore brought forward in the written Word to function as epiphanies for the listening church. This is their role today as it was in the first century; the stories themselves, as living Word of God, are manifestations of the glory of the only begotten Son.

In the story of the epiphany at the river, we read that John the Baptist immediately recognized Jesus as the long-expected Messiah of Israel. Each of the four evangelists dramatizes this recognition. In the three Synoptic Gospels, John says, "He who is coming after me is mightier than I, whose sandals I am not worthy to unloose." John's fiery preaching links the appearance at the River Jordan with the apocalyptic pronouncement that the Messiah's coming signifies the turn of the ages.[3] The effects of the final judgment of God upon sin are already manifest in his earthly coming, as John makes clear in his take-no-prisoners preaching: "Even now the axe is laid to the root of the trees; every tree therefore that does not bear good fruit is cut down and thrown into the fire" (Luke 3:9).

Understanding the baptism of Jesus, then, requires us to give full attention to the preaching of John. John is quite specifically linked to the Old Testament prophets in the Gospels. He is described in all three Synoptics as the one of whom Isaiah spoke: a voice crying in the wilderness, "Prepare the way of the Lord, / Make straight in the desert a highway for our God" (Isaiah 40:3). In Matthew he is clearly envisioned as Elijah *redivivus*, emerging from the wilderness wearing a camel pelt for clothing and eating wild honey (Matthew 3:4). It is said moreover that "all Judea" came out to hear John's apocalyptic preaching: "He who is coming after me . . . will baptize you with the Holy Spirit and with fire. His winnowing fork is in his hand, and he will clear his threshing floor and gather his wheat into the granary, but the chaff he will burn with unquenchable fire" (Matthew 3:11-12).

These evocations of the Day of Judgment are not a peculiarity of John the Baptist. Jesus' own apocalyptic announcements are front and center on the first Sunday in Advent, when the lectionary always features the "Synoptic apocalypse."[4] The point being made here is that the arrival of Jesus Messiah is the first event of the age to come. That is part of the context for Jesus' somewhat cryptic saying that his submission to baptism is "to fulfill all righteousness" (Matthew 3:15). Such fulfillment will be the sign that the kingdom of God is already present.[5]

Understanding the baptism of Jesus involves some understanding of the prophetic tradition. In the post-Exilic prophets Daniel, Zephaniah, Zechariah, and Malachi, there is a quite startling shift of emphasis from human history, which offers no permanent hope, to the coming Day of the Lord—a climactic event of final judgment when all wrongs will be redressed, and God's reign of righteousness will be established forever. John the Baptizer fits squarely within this tradition, and indeed personifies its actual arrival, as Jesus himself says later: "Truly, I say to you, among those born of women there has risen no one greater than John the Baptist" (Matthew 11:11).[6]

These themes are prominent in the three Synoptic Gospels. The Fourth Gospel, typically, tells the story in a different way; the evangelist John had his own special sources. His capsule concerning the baptism is striking—not only because it is repeated twice in one chapter, but also because John the Baptist in John's Gospel, in just a few words, twice gathers a vast amount of scriptural and theological resonance into one image: "Behold, the Lamb of God, who takes away the sin of the world!" (John 1:29; see also 1:36). This pronouncement, deeply rooted in the archetypal story of the Passover lamb, has been prominent in the church throughout its history. It reappears at the end of the Scriptures in the Johannine book of Revelation, where Christ appears as the Lamb "standing, as though it had been slain" (Revelation 5:6) and "slain from the foundation of the world" (Revelation 13:8 KJV). The epiphany at the baptism, when all four Gospels are taken into account, manifests Jesus in many of his overlapping identities: as the Messiah of Israel long prophesied, as the eschatological judge who is to come in the Day of the Lord, as the sacrificed Passover lamb who is slain for the feast taken in haste on the eve of the exodus from exile, and by extension the scapegoat in the wilderness who bears away the sins of the chosen people (Leviticus 16:8-10, 20-22). The depth and breadth of the biblical imagery gathered together in this single epiphany by the River Jordan is extraordinary.

Any preacher or teacher called to interpret the baptism of Jesus on the first Sunday after January 6 has a mighty task. At the very least, the powerful words of the Baptizer in Matthew and Luke as he evokes the final judgment, or Day of the Lord, should not be allowed to drift by as though they were too hot to handle.[7] They prefigure many of the teachings of Jesus himself about the judgment of God.[8] It is imperative to understand that the one doing the teaching about the day of reckoning is the very same one who will take the final judgment upon himself, as the sacrificed Lamb.

Taking all four Gospel witnesses together, there are two things going on at once here—the individual and the cosmic. To be baptized by John is to submit to a personal, individual cleansing from sin. But who is able to take away the sin of the whole world? Repeat that question to yourself, reader, and you will see why the baptism of Jesus must be an epiphany of one who has a unique destiny and unique power. Each evangelist attests that John recognized that unique person instantly. This is a powerful sign of the prophetic gift from God that leads John to say, "He must increase, but I must decrease" (John 3:30).

So, in all four accounts of the baptism, Jesus is seen as the Lamb of God who takes upon himself the double weight of sin:

- As responsible human guilt from which we must be cleansed (as by water—John 13:8)

- As the adversarial cosmic power from which we must be delivered (as by fire—Matthew 3:11)

The second person of the Trinity has arrived in human flesh to accomplish both of these impossibilities. God in three Persons is determined to do this in human flesh, undergoing the immolation that we could not. Thus Paul shows how Jesus brings us in baptism through death into life (Romans 6:3-4).

Of the three Synoptic versions of the baptism, Matthew's is the fullest. It is the only account that includes this exchange between John and Jesus:

> John would have prevented him, saying, "I need to be baptized by you, and do you come to me?" But Jesus answered him, "Let it be so now; for thus it is fitting for us to fulfil all righteousness." Then [John] consented. (Matthew 3:14-15)

The early church almost certainly had difficulty explaining why Jesus, the Son of God and sinless one, had submitted to baptism. It surely would have been easier just to omit mention of it. However, it must have been a well-known fact, since John the Baptist had been a notable public figure in very recent memory. Matthew surely intends to shed light on the problem of Jesus being baptized by quoting Jesus' intention, but the somewhat enigmatic utterance of Jesus has been a subject of some perplexity. What does he mean, "to fulfil all righteousness"?

Paul the apostle and John the fourth evangelist both come into the conversation here about the fulfillment of "all righteousness." It is in Paul's letters—especially Romans—that we see clearly how two English words are used to translate the single Greek word *dikaiosyne*. Those two words are "justice" and "righteousness." This should be a foundation stone of every Bible reader's understanding.[9] Some translations use "justice" more often than "righteousness," which can be helpful in underscoring God's commitment to "justice in the gate," both here in this life and even more, ultimate justice in the age to come.[10] Jesus is not interested in personal righteousness only. His mission is world-transformative, delivering human institutions from bondage to the demonic powers.

In the sub-apostolic period, the biblical scene of the baptism of Jesus was interpreted mythologically as a descent into the realm of death and Satan. By his immersion, the waters are purified and the demons conquered. Those who are baptized, therefore, share in his victory over the powers of darkness (as in the baptismal hymn in

Colossians 1:13—"He has delivered us from the dominion of darkness and transferred us to the kingdom of his beloved Son"). Thus the baptismal story is linked to the descent into hell.[11] There is strong biblical warrant for this interpretation in Romans 6:1-11, where Paul affirms that the Christian is baptized not only into Christ's literal death but also into a death to sin.

There is a powerful carving of the baptism on the doors of the church of Saint Maria im Kapitol in Cologne, depicting Christ coming up out of the water, still half-submerged, with the dove of the Spirit alight on his head—and a demon prostrate in the water under his feet. This imagery should be better known. The baptism of Jesus was an engagement with "sin, death, and the devil"—alternatively, with "the world, the flesh, and the devil." As he rises from the water, his victory over the demonic realm is enacted, as the carving signifies. Jesus' ministry following the baptism will consist of many exorcisms, demonstrating his lordship over the demonic world. The utterly unexpected reversal comes when, in his Passion, Christ deliberately submits to his suffering and death, putting himself under the power of the devil. This is what it took to "fulfil all righteousness."

John's incendiary preaching conjures up the one who will wield God's "winnowing fork" on the last day, gathering up the wheat and burning the chaff "with unquenchable fire" (Matthew 3:12). It is tempting to identify Jesus right away as the one with the fork, but he will follow a quite unexpected path. In all the Gospels as they unfold, he will clearly identify himself as the One who is to come (*ho erchomenos*; see Revelation 1:4) but it will become apparent as we follow him into Lent and Passiontide that he will relinquish his power as the reaper and will make common cause with the chaff—which is all of us.

This is a good place to address the theme of *recapitulation*, firmly planted in the great tradition by Irenaeus in the second century. It is founded in the story told by Paul in Romans 5. Because it is so important to Paul, he retells the story six times in six separate sentences! Here's just one of them:

> As one man's [Adam's] trespass led to condemnation for all men, so one man's [Jesus'] act of righteousness leads to acquittal and life for all men. (Romans 5:18)

Paul then writes definitively to the Romans, "We were buried therefore with him *by baptism* into death, so that as Christ was raised from the dead *by the glory of the Father*, we too might walk in newness of life" (Romans 6:4).

The baptisms of believers would be victory celebrations and the church would be renewed if these biblical passages and others like them were made a standard part of every Christian's knowledge and faith.

Baptisms on the First Sunday After the Epiphany

The church has made this day a premier day for baptisms, second only to the Easter Vigil. Teaching about the meaning of the sacrament should be the first order of the day, but all too often, baptisms (at any time of year) are performed perfunctorily, with parents and godparents unprepared for their responses, and in the case of infant baptism the congregation is typically more attentive to the cuteness (or misbehavior) of the little ones being baptized than to the momentous change of dominion that is being effected.[12] This transfer of power is expounded in a striking passage widely believed to be a portion of a baptismal liturgy in the early church:

[We give] thanks to the Father, who has qualified us to share in the inheritance of the saints in light. He has delivered us from the dominion of darkness and transferred us to the kingdom of his beloved Son, in whom we have redemption, the forgiveness of sins. (Colossians 1:12-14)

If adults are being baptized, it is all the more important to stress that a new life under a new lordship has begun. Paul's impassioned teaching about baptism should be part of every baptismal catechism: "Do you not know that all of us who have been baptized into Christ Jesus were baptized into his death? . . . So you also must consider yourselves dead to sin and alive to God in Christ Jesus. . . . Yield yourselves to God as men who have been brought from death to life, and your members to God as [God's] instruments of righteousness" (Romans 6:3, 11-13).

As Paul specifically says, the glory (*doxa*) of the Father accomplishes this. The Epiphany season taken as a whole affords a special opportunity to teach the trajectory of the entire history of Jesus, the incarnate Son of the Father. The plotting of the season, described in these pages, sets before us the ministry and teaching of Jesus told in highlights as he moves inexorably to his Passion and death.

This particular Sunday—the baptism of our Lord—commemorates a foundational event that was specifically connected to Epiphany as far back as we can trace it. Therefore it is of great importance that the day should take on a special solemnity as well as great joy. The sacrament of baptism should be brought forward and made central on this day, with emphasis on the gospel teaching that baptism recapitulates the passage through death to life for each baptizand. It can't be emphasized too often: this is the center of Christian faith and life.

Returning to our theme of *epiphaneia* as the manifestation of Christ's glory, we can hardly do better than to look at the passage from Isaiah that is always appointed to be read on the Sunday commemorating the baptism of Jesus. Notice especially the interplay between justice and righteousness (the same word in Hebrew). This is emphasized here, because if it were to be well understood in our churches, we would not have such a dire chasm between social and individual righteousness.

> Behold my servant, whom I uphold,
>   my chosen, in whom my soul delights;
> I have put my Spirit upon him . . .
>   he will faithfully bring forth *justice*.

He will not fail or be discouraged
    till he has established *justice* in the earth;
    and the coastlands wait for his law.

Thus says God, the Lord . . .
"I am the Lord, I have called you in *righteousness*. . . .
I have given you as a covenant to the people,
    a light to the nations. . . .
Behold, the former things have come to pass,
    and new things I now declare;
before they spring forth
    I tell you of them." (Isaiah 42:1-10)

This is an inspired choice from the Old Testament for this day in the calendar. In no uncertain terms, this prophecy of Isaiah—one of the four "servant" passages in Isaiah 10–55—is annealed to the appearance of Jesus at Jordan. The Father declares that this is the long-awaited servant of the Lord, the one whose coming is, precisely, the "new thing"—the light to the nations (the Gentiles), the Presentation, and the eschatological giver of justice and righteousness (again, it is the same word in both Hebrew and Greek).

If only one thing can be accomplished in a baptismal sermon during this season, it should be the *epiphaneia* of

Jesus Christ. The famous hymn "Joy to the World," by the esteemed hymn writer Isaac Watts, expresses the theme of the Epiphany season in a single verse:

> He rules the world with truth and grace,
> And makes the nations prove
> The glories of his righteousness
> And wonders of his love.[13]

As we arrive at the chapters on Jesus' ministry and teachings, we will see how the Epiphany season tells us of *both* "the glories of his righteousness" *and* the "wonders of his love."

6

The Wine

The story of the wine at the wedding in Cana is unique to the Gospel of John. This story was associated with the season following the Feast of the Epiphany from the earliest centuries of the church. We have already quoted the key verse that identifies the marriage feast at Cana as an early manifestation of the identity of Jesus. John is careful to deploy this identification at the outset to emphasize its importance as an *epiphaneia*:

> This, the first of his signs, Jesus did at Cana in Galilee, and *manifested his glory*; and his disciples believed in him. (John 2:11)

The sequence of readings in the Epiphany season is worth noting. The baptism comes first, then the miracle at Cana—the first "sign" (*semeion*), to use John's distinctive word. When the Matthew-Mark-Luke versions of the baptism are set alongside John's story of the wine at the wedding, there are some special features to be noted.

First, at the wedding, Jesus *manifests himself*. This is different from the baptismal accounts, where God the Father is the revelatory speaker. In the Synoptic narratives of the baptism, an emerging theology of the Trinity can be detected. The Father and the Son act as one, and the descent of the dove testifies to the Three in One. Thus, the Epiphany season is, among many other things, trinitarian. At Cana, the baptismal manifestations are greatly enlarged. At the baptism, Jesus is the *recipient* of the Father's words and action. At Cana, however, *he himself* performs a public action. He does not need to say that the authority of the Father is at work; we already know that Jesus and the Father are one (John 1:1).

The second feature is the *effect* of the miracle. The wedding guests observe Jesus' command and taste the miraculous wine, but the fourth evangelist structures his story so as to put the emphasis on the really significant effect of this "first of his signs"—namely, that his disciples beheld it and believed in him. Clearly this is meant as an appeal not only to John's contemporary readers, but also to listeners throughout the ages and to this day, for the entire Epiphany season is an extended invitation to behold and believe.[1]

A third feature is that in the case of the marriage at Cana, the fourth evangelist anticipates the hallowed imagery of Jesus as the one who will be the bridegroom of his bride the church—an identification that has been strengthened by centuries of study of the Song of Songs.[2] The marriage service in the 1928 Book of Common Prayer makes a lovely reference to the Cana story:

> Dearly beloved, we are gathered together here in the sight of God, and in the face of this company, to join together this man and this woman in holy matrimony, which is an honorable estate, instituted by God, and signifying unto us the mystical union that is between Christ and his Church: which holy estate Christ adorned and beautified with his presence and first miracle that he wrought in Cana of Galilee.[3]

There is a fourth feature. The words about matrimony are much to be cherished, but they do not by any means convey the central message of the Cana story itself. There is a different reference that holds a key to John's narrative. The image of a great feast (and no other feast in the ancient Near East excelled a wedding feast, which could go on for days) is prominent in the Old Testament, where it often takes on the character of the messianic feast in the Day of the Lord. Thus, as the guests drink the wine that Jesus has produced, the host says, "You have kept the best wine for the last." This is related to the promise of God in the book of Isaiah:

> On this mountain the Lord of hosts will make for
>   all peoples
>   a feast of rich food, a feast of well-aged wines,
>   of rich food filled with marrow, of well-aged
>   wines strained clear.
> And he will destroy on this mountain
>   the shroud that is cast over all peoples,
>   the covering that is spread over all nations;
>   he will swallow up death forever. (Isaiah 25:6-8,
>   NRSV)[4]

Thus the marriage at Cana can readily be seen as a reflection of the Old Testament image of the lavish heavenly banquet in the City of God in the eschatological future, a pledge of God's faithfulness to his promise of release from the curse that has been "cast over all peoples"—the captivity that Paul will describe as bondage to Sin and Death. This, too, is part of the rich background of John's narrative.

The Cana story is not told as a historian or a biographer would tell it. John's purpose, as throughout his Gospel, is theological.[5] The miracle of the water and wine is the first of Jesus' "signs" in John's book. It offers the first glimpse of Jesus' glory. Rudolf Bultmann observes that Jesus' *doxa*, though often thought of as "a shining light or substance," is in fact twofold: it is the Son's *mode of being*, and it is equally his *mode of operation* in creation—as in the creation of new wine.[6] Christ's mode of *being* is that of the second person of the Trinity. His mode of *operation* is his active power. The Cana miracle is open to sentimentalization (how nice that Jesus wanted everyone to be happy!) but the evangelist's emphasis is on his power of command and his intense sense of purpose.[7]

Therefore Jesus' much-discussed response to his mother redirects their dialogue to the *telos* (the divinely appointed purpose or end) that John has in mind: "My hour has not yet come" (John 2:4).[8] Throughout the Fourth Gospel the evangelist repeatedly refers to Jesus' "hour," which does not actually arrive until he purposefully turns to the cross ("The hour has come for the Son of man to be glorified," John 12:23). There is no doubt about what the evangelist has in mind here. His purpose is twofold: to declare Jesus' *doxa* so as to elicit faith, and to point ahead to *the hour of glory*, that is, the cross. The "hour" is not a day on the calendar. It is the time of the fulfillment of Jesus' destiny, so that when his sacrifice is completed, "it is finished" and his *doxa* is finally and fully revealed, in all its paradox of suffering and victory. All of this is foreshadowed in the Cana miracle.

There are many directions to go in preaching and teaching this "sign" at Cana. It is a sign of God's absolute power over the animate and inanimate creation. It is a sign of God's exuberant and prodigal generosity.[9] It is certainly not wrong to mention Jesus' adorning the institution of marriage with his presence and his actions, but this is not the central message of the evangelist. The central purpose is to do what the season of Epiphany does—to reveal the glory of Jesus as the one who spreads out a heavenly feast.

John emphasizes the lavish nature of the gift of wine, and makes a point of saying that the massive wine jars were filled "to the brim" by the servants. This indicates the overflowing nature of God's generosity and links us also with Old Testament passages about the coming kingdom of God. There is another echo here of Isaiah: "There is an outcry in the streets for lack of wine" (Isaiah 24:11), which is followed by the divine promise: when the anointed one comes, there will be no more deprivation, for the Lord will reign on Mount Zion and "he will manifest his glory" (Isaiah 24:23). This is the end-of-time future foreseen by the prophet, when God's inexhaustible bounty will be poured out upon his redeemed people.

A noted Johannine scholar sets John's use of *doxa* (glory) in proximity to Paul's commanding word *dunamis*:

> [Jesus'] power is so much part of his nature that the evangelist finds it more correct to adopt a term which expresses *both* the nature of God as it manifests itself *and* his mighty action, "radiant brightness" and "powerful activity" [*dunamis*] notions already combined in the Old Testament. . . .
>
> In the divinely-wrought event [at Cana], the believer experiences something of the divine being of Jesus, contemplates the majesty of the Son of God and also senses the brightness of the heavenly world which he cannot yet see with his bodily eyes.[10]

All of this is summed up in the evangelist's words, "This, the first of his signs, Jesus did at Cana in Galilee, and manifested his glory [*doxa*], and his disciples believed in him" (John 2:11). John is not at all interested in what the other guests at the wedding might have thought. He wants those who hear the retelling in generations yet to come to understand that the central message here is the call to faith in Jesus, a message that was received by those called to be his disciples, and that they recognized his "glory."

That should be the concern of all who preach and bear witness to Jesus, at all times of the year, but with special intention during this season of epiphanies. There will always be those who do not recognize him, but they will nevertheless be in his sight and have a part in his eternal plan (see Romans 11). The church, however, in its observance of Epiphany, is to take care of its calling: to point to Christ's glory, and let his glory take care of itself.

7

The Ministry

In our time, it has become increasingly common to hear church leaders in the mainline denominations present Jesus variously as a healer, a moral teacher, a lover of outcasts, a political revolutionary, a threat to "institutional" religion, a spiritual guide, an example to emulate, and to be sure a numinous personality—but not as the Son of God, the judge who is to come, the Lord of the cosmos, the second person of the blessed Trinity. Will Willimon has often said that the problem with the "Jesus scholars" is that they seem to work under the assumption that Jesus is dead. Nowadays, the mainline churches often seem timid about proclaiming him as our living Lord, as though we were embarrassed to claim too much. Perhaps we ourselves have not altogether seen his glory and come to believe in him as did the disciples at table with him in Cana.

In this chapter, we arrive at the Gospel accounts of Jesus' public ministry, and the listening church hears of his glory in various scenes related by the evangelists to illustrate his identity as Messiah of Israel and Lord of the Gentiles. In a time when the name of Jesus Christ is more often than not used as an expletive, Christians need confidence in the identity of our Lord and master. We need to read the Bible more carefully, listening for the way that the witnesses to Jesus seek to convey his glory in their accounts of his ministry, death, and resurrection. The season of Epiphany is designed to display just that.

Of first importance (though often ignored) is the fact that in each of the three Synoptic Gospels, Jesus' public ministry begins with his confrontations with the demonic powers.[1] In the earliest Gospel, the very first public action of Jesus is an exorcism (Mark 1:23-27). This is enormously significant. The incarnate Son of God did not arrive in peaceful neutral territory, but in a world under occupation. If Jesus' identity is to be fully displayed, then his power and authority over the demonic dimension has to be established. There is no New Testament without the rampaging adversary of God, the would-be destroyer of all of God's purposes. In the New Testament, this adversary is called by various names: the devil, Satan, Beelzebub, the ruler of this world, the prince of the power of the air, the spirit at work in the sons of disobedience. Paul has his own way of identifying this demonic realm: he calls it the reign of Sin and Death, which holds humankind and all creation in bondage; without this scenario, Paul's message loses its radical edge (see for instance Romans 6 and 7, which cannot be understood without the looming presence of Sin and Death understood as great powers).

Next to God himself, the "ruler of this world" (John 12:31) is more powerful than any other entity in heaven or on earth. In Christ, however, God brings judgment upon the world and will finally destroy this usurper. This New Testament cosmology is essential in order to understand what Jesus' *doxa* really amounts to, and no account of the life of Jesus is adequate without it. In Matthew, the first thing Jesus does after his baptism is to contend with the devil in the wilderness. Thus Matthew sets the stage; there is no ministry of Jesus without this struggle. Christ's conquest of Satan in this scene is complete, if provisional; as Luke tells us, Satan will return at "an opportune time" (Luke 4:13), and we are to understand that to be Gethsemane, when Jesus enters into his final battle.[2] Luke has an important place in the depiction of this essential confrontation as it happens during the ministry; it is in Luke that Jesus envisions Satan falling "like lightning from heaven" (Luke 10:18). John, as usual, comes at this another way, telling how Jesus calls Satan "the ruler of this world" who "has no power over me" (John 14:30).

All of this undergirds the various epiphanies of Jesus' divine sovereignty that we see in the lectionary readings. In this sense, the Epiphany season is preparing us for the seasons that follow. Without the distillation of Jesus' authority, majesty, power, and divine identity that we see in these six to eight weeks, the move from Christmas to Lent and Holy Week loses its grounding in the incarnate divine purpose.

The subsequent actions and teachings of Jesus should be understood in this light: the gradual revelation of his being. Without these epiphanies, no matter how admirable or how worthy of emulation Jesus may be, he becomes indistinguishable from other prominent religious leaders such as the Dalai Lama. It is in knowing Jesus as the Son, transcendently unique in his relationship to God the Father, that we come truly to follow him as participants in his victory over Sin and Death.[3]

The calling of Jesus' disciples is a case in point, and it is one of the leading motifs in the Epiphany lectionary (cycles A and B). It is common to hear sermons about Jesus' "invitation" to the fishermen on the shore of the Sea of Galilee. We are urged to respond to his "invitation" to become his disciples. This is to miss the point. As Jesus walks along the beach and sees the men with their boats, he utters not an invitation, but a command: "Follow me." Mark, typically, dramatizes this as an offer they can't refuse: "Immediately they left their nets and followed him" (Mark 1:18). Likewise Matthew:

> [Jesus] saw a man called Matthew sitting at the tax office; and he said to him, "Follow me." And he rose and followed him. (Matthew 9:9)

Just like that. In Caravaggio's masterpiece *The Calling of Saint Matthew*, Jesus enters the room where the tax collectors are counting money, and we see him commanding, "Follow me." As he says this, he points to Matthew. Matthew gestures, "Who, me?" Jesus' feet are already turned back toward the door; there is no possibility of

Matthew refusing. On another occasion Jesus seems to offer an invitation to a rich young man who "went away sorrowful" (Matthew 19:22). Apparently Jesus can choose either to invite or more forcefully to command according to his own mysterious purposes, for he says afterward, "With God all things are possible" (Matthew 19:26).

An epiphany in the New Testament is a revelation of Jesus' identity and power. He is able both to command and to elicit an immediate response. This is not just personal charisma. At the baptism we have heard the voice of God identifying his Son. We are meant to be awestruck by these indications of Jesus' majesty. That is what the season of Epiphany is designed to display.

In year C, the Epiphany lectionary includes Luke 4:21-32, the inaugural sermon in the synagogue at Nazareth. Following the temptation by Satan in the wilderness,

> Jesus returned in the *power* of the Spirit into Galilee, and a report concerning him went out through all the surrounding country. And he taught in their synagogues, being *glorified* by all.

Note the words that we have been emphasizing. *Dunamis* (power—a favored word of the apostle Paul) and *doxa*

(glory-fied) are used to make the strongest possible impression of Jesus' singular persona.

In the late 1960s and continuing on to this day, the
words of Jesus on that occasion in the synagogue have
functioned for many as a canon within the canon. He
takes the scroll of the book of Isaiah and reads aloud:

> The Spirit of the Lord is upon me,
> because he has anointed me to preach good news
>   to the poor.
> He has sent me to proclaim release to the captives
> and recovering of sight to the blind,
> to set at liberty those who are oppressed,
> to proclaim the acceptable year of the Lord.
>   (Luke 4: 18-19)

To be sure, it is not wrong to emphasize the content of
this passage from the great prophet Isaiah. It conveys a
central message of God's deliverance to those who are
captive, without power. In no way should this be de-
emphasized or passed over. However, the main thrust of
the narrative, when seen in the context of Luke's account
of the inaugural ministry, does not lie so much with
Isaiah as it does with the messianic implications. The

overwhelming impression of the passage in its setting is that of Jesus' self-disclosure:

> And he closed the book, and gave it back to the attendant, and sat down; and the eyes of all in the synagogue were fixed on him. And he began to say to them, "Today this scripture has been fulfilled in your hearing." (Luke 4:20)

This is equivalent to saying, "I am the Messiah." It is an epiphany. Luke means it that way. Jesus' announcement should never be detached from its framing. His next words to the listeners ("No prophet is acceptable in his own country," Luke 4:24) are a barely disguised assault upon the smug congregation and its leaders, so deliberately provocative that they rise up and try to lynch him.

We know from the story of the baptism that the way to receive the coming of Messiah Jesus is to kneel and receive the forgiveness of sins. The reaction of the congregation at Nazareth is the opposite. Luke has told this story of the rejection at the synagogue to let us know that this Messiah is going to be lethally controversial. He is already looking ahead to the Passion narrative. But the revelatory focus on Jesus' identity does not subside; the very next thing that happens in Luke's Gospel is that Jesus goes down into Capernaum where "they were astonished at his teaching, for his word was with authority" (Luke 4:32) and he performs a dramatic exorcism. These appearances, these words and these deeds, are epiphanies. Any interpretation of Jesus' words in Luke 4:21-32 that omits or downplays the disclosure of who Jesus is and where his power comes from is a failure to "preach good news to the poor."

In year B, Mark's year, there is room in the lectionary for two of Jesus' remarkable healings—those of a leper, the ultimate pariah in biblical times, and a helpless paralyzed man let down through the roof. It is well known, even by those who know little of Jesus, that he healed sick people; what is not necessarily known is that the extraordinary healings display his divine power and glory. In Mark, the healings are told as epiphanies—divine revelations of his unique status.

The outcast leper seems to know Jesus' power, kneeling before him and saying to him that he knows he can heal him (see Mark 1:40-45)—thus the evangelist conveys a message to all who hear the story. Mark puts this power into even sharper focus when Jesus is confronted by the paralyzed man let down through the roof. Instead of healing the man, Jesus says to him that his sins are forgiven. He then asks those standing around, "Which is easier, to say to the paralytic, 'Your sins are forgiven,' or to say, 'Rise, take up your pallet and walk'? But so that you may know that the Son of man has authority on earth to forgive sins"—he turns again to the paralyzed man— "Rise, take up your pallet, and go home" (Mark 2:9-10). Mark ends this narrative with, "They were all amazed and glorified God, saying, 'We never saw anything like this!'" (Mark 2:12; see also Matthew 9:1-8).

It is important to understand that the stories of Jesus' miraculous healings in the four Gospels are focused on the reactions of the onlookers. In our own day, believers are confronted daily with the fact that healings do not always occur. In their way of telling these stories, the evangelists have made clear that the miraculous cures themselves, while they certainly show God's special care and love for the afflicted, are not the central point. What is on display in all the miracle stories is the glory of Jesus and his power to show it or withhold it according to the divine will of the Father—which is his will also. Thus the power and the glory of the message of Epiphany is moving ever deeper into the season.[4]

8

The Teaching

How does the theme of glory that predominates in Epiphany fit with the large amount of space devoted to the Sermon on the Mount during the season?[1]

It all depends on what one means by *glory*. The "glory, glory, hallelujah" chorus of the "Battle Hymn of the Republic" is fun to sing, but it is not such a good thing to confuse military glory, or patriotic glory, or even the glory of a righteous cause, with the glory that belongs solely to Jesus Christ. Claiming all the glory for one side in a battle—even in such "righteous" wars as the American Civil War or World War II—leads to the dangers of idolatry and a facile demonization of one's enemies.[2] The way of life described by Jesus in the Sermon on the Mount is antithetical to that. It is the way of life that he himself lived, the only human being to do so perfectly. His was a life led entirely for others, in a way that no other human being has ever been able to do. His glory is that of perfected humanity, the new Adam who has relived the life of the old Adam, and in doing so gave up everything in a way no human ever has, for a result unachievable by any other person. The way of the sermon and his identity as its giver and enabler led to his death at the hands of his enemies in the ultimate exchange—"the righteous for the unrighteous" (1 Peter 3:18).

Almost from its beginnings in the power of the resurrection of the crucified Lord, the church has recognized the Sermon on the Mount as the radical center of Jesus' teaching. But it is strange teaching. It seems to be a manifesto of humility and self-sacrifice. The way of life that it describes does not seem in the least to fit with the theme of glory. On the contrary, it seems to require a renunciation of glory as the world understands it. Some of it seems humanly impossible, or humanly impracticable at the least. Yet the position of the Gospel of Matthew at the head of the New Testament, the first of the four Gospels, is in no small degree owing to the early recognition of Matthew's extended version of the sermon. It is the sine qua non of Christian discipleship, a summons to be an embodied enactment of the Way of God. Its glory is in its overturning of every human pretension as it incarnates in words the lived life of Jesus. As such it is his gift to all who love him and seek to follow him. It is the Way of glory.

It may be doubted, however, how seriously the ordinary Christian takes the Sermon on the Mount, or how well the average churchgoer even knows it. How many preachers have expounded the whole of it, or sought to illustrate what it might look like in practice? As soon as we ask this question, we must acknowledge that there has always been a tension in the way the sermon has been interpreted, sometimes rising to the level of serious divisions in Christian theology. Are we to understand the Sermon on the Mount as law, or as gospel?

Like the Ten Commandments, the sermon can be read as *prescriptive* instead of *descriptive*. When that occurs, the liberating gospel of unconditional grace is obscured under a heavy weight of impossible expectation. The result will often be that the sermon is not taken seriously. Preachers and teachers will always need to be alert to the challenge of getting this balance right. It is always tempting to read the Epistle of James prescriptively ("Faith by itself, if it has no works, is dead," James 2:17) without reference to Paul ("No human being will be justified in his sight by works of the law," Romans 3:20).[3] Paul's fundamental emphasis on justifying faith is not contradicted by the works that arise organically out of that faith, for the true vine produces branches (John 15:1-9; see also Romans 11:17-24). James seems to be saying that over a long lifetime, such as that of Abraham (James 2:21-23), God's free gift of justifying faith will plainly show itself in God's own works of righteousness. God's mercy is fathomless, but it will never cancel out his justice; this seeming contradiction must continue to be at the heart of any serious attempt to proclaim the gospel. The symbiotic relationship of righteousness and mercy lies at the heart of the Beatitudes and the rest of the Sermon on the Mount, and they serve to authenticate faith. This understanding of faith and works should not be understood as a threat to the radicality of Paul's preaching about the justification of the ungodly (Romans 4:5; 5:6). There are certain qualities that will emerge in the person who knows herself to be justified by grace and faith alone (*sola gratia, sola fidei*). Those qualities will be a *result*, not a *cause* of justification. Such qualities will look like the Beatitudes appearing in that person, even though the great adversary will be pulling in the other direction until the Lord comes again.

If the Sermon on the Mount is preached and taught without context, as if James had contradicted Paul, then the life of faith is no longer understood to be a gift, but a human achievement, and will either feel like a burden of impossibility or, conversely, a source of smug self-righteousness. In either case, such teaching is not the gospel. Therefore the preaching should never sound pre-scriptive. It can and should be powerfully illustrated, minus the hortatory quality that undermines the motivation of those who are weak in faith—or that, contrarily, fortifies those who project an air of being among the righteous.[4]

Flannery O'Connor's short story "Revelation" comes to mind. The central character, Ruby Turpin, is a good woman. She has always been certain of her place in society and therefore of her salvation. She is therefore amazed (and transfigured) when she receives a vision of herself and her husband entering into glory at the very tail end of the parade of saints, far behind the "White trash" that she has always regarded as vastly inferior to herself.

It has been rightly said that the Beatitudes that introduce the Sermon on the Mount are not exhortations but congratulations. They are in the present tense, implying that they are already taking shape in those who would be disciples of Jesus. There is something here of *logizomai*, that key word in the preaching of Saint Paul often translated as "reckoned": "Abraham believed God, and it was *reckoned* to him as righteousness" (Romans 4:3). This *reckoning* is the work of God alone. Another way of putting this is the often-heard "become what you already are." That slogan has come in for its share of ridicule, but it is nevertheless true of the way that God justifies sinners. It is quite different from "fake it till you make it," which is cynical in its purpose, lacking in any affirmation of the power of the God who calls sinners to righteousness and works in them to create that righteousness. "Become what you already are" is an affirmation of the action of the one who reckons (*logizomai*, to count as) sinners as righteous. It is a particularly apt paraphrase of the Beatitudes. "Blessed are those who hunger and thirst for righteousness" (Matthew 5:6) is illustrative of the Epiphany theme of the glory of God's righteousness making itself known in the most unlikely vessels. Thus the disciples of Jesus participate in his glory in spite of themselves.

In the story of the miracle of the wine at Cana, the evangelist John wants us to see that the glory of Jesus is defined, in large measure, by his power. He is able to change water into fine wine with a word. His glory is manifest in everything he says and does, whether it is noticed by multitudes or only by a few. His power is fully and completely that of the Creator of the universe; if it is muted, withheld, or hidden at times in his incarnate life, it is because he chooses it to be—only in his Passion does he entirely give up his powers in self-sacrifice. The Sermon on the Mount is his tapestry of power woven together with love. It is a fully realized depiction of human life with the Godhead at the loom. Its glory is the Son's own self, the new Adam incarnate and free from the power of sin. If this is difficult to imagine, fallen human nature being as wayward and corrupt as it is, then we need always to recall *the power of his glory* that can overcome every obstacle to its realization in the eternal life that he gives.

The way of life Jesus describes in the sermon is therefore that of his own body, the church. The sermon is not a manifesto for the way that the world at large is supposed to work in this "present evil age" (Galatians 1:4). It is above all a description of the way of life that the disciples of Jesus are to embody in their communities. Richard Lischer, emeritus professor at Duke Divinity School with a high degree of commitment to the health of local congregations, has powerfully pursued this fundamental insight. The sermon is meant to shape and nurture the life of the Christian fellowship. Lischer's descriptions of how this should work in the church are arresting: instead of training its members to be on committees, he writes, the pastors and leaders of congregations would be training the congregation to be pastors, "caring for one another in the stress and conflict of daily life."[5] To the points made in these pages, Lischer writes that the liturgy of the church presupposes the kind of community that is nurtured by the Sermon on the Mount:

> It presupposed an ordered and intense process of formation directed by those who are mature in faith, for the purpose of godly thought and behavior. . . . Its end is not personal happiness or fulfillment but "the Day of Jesus Christ," which is the same End for which the Sermon on the Mount was given to the church.[6]

And so the sermon's way of life is profoundly secure in the promised end when the Lord of creation is victor. It is a depiction of the sort of life that is his own to give. It will therefore always be open to multiple misinterpretations by those who do not understand the giver. And yet the sermon is not esoteric. It is not hidden, not a gnostic secret accessible only to a few. It is open and available to the world and stands in its own irreducible power, free to anyone who would embrace it. It is intended in particular, however, for those who are branches of the living who says, "Apart from me you can do nothing" (John 15:5). Therefore, all attempts to file the sermon away as naively impracticable are fatal misunderstandings of what it is and by Whom it is enabled. To anyone who tries that, the Lord says, "You know neither the scriptures nor the power of God" (Matthew 22:29). Thus Lischer writes:

> There can be no fitting conclusion to the study of a living eschatological document. The Sermon belongs to the pilgrim church. . . . No individual has ever captured its definitive meaning, for as the expression of God's radical pastoral care, the Sermon on the Mount can only be "interpreted" as communities of Christians attempt to live it.[7]

The Bruderhof is one such Christian community with many locations around the world. Unlike most such attempts to build radical communities, the Bruderhof has not only survived, it is thriving. In 2021 they celebrated their hundredth anniversary. Its members are committed to live according to the Sermon on the Mount and, significantly, to personify the description of the earliest Christian communities in Acts 4:32-37.[8] Their openness to society at large ("in" it but not "of" it) is remarkable; many of them are out in the world from time to time, serving among unaffiliated others with a surprising level of comfort; they are exceptionally affirming of those not similarly committed, with a minimum of self-righteousness—making them attractive to seekers. Unlike monastic orders and the all-but-vanished Shakers, they are more often than not married, with families of (typically) more than two children who are lovingly raised and educated within the community. Unlike the Amish, they are at home on social media and make good use of it.[9] They earn enough money from their shared businesses of making beautifully crafted wooden toys and sophisticated medical equipment to have a presence in the world at large, but there is no private ownership; all is shared within the community.

The Bruderhof is proof that the Sermon on the Mount can actually be lived, and far from being a rebuke to the rest of us, they are a great encouragement.[10] Not many are called to their radical way of life, but their effect on those who encounter them is considerable. It goes without saying that they are not perfect, and have their struggles, but their continuing existence, their influence, and their strength are a powerful witness to the rest of us that the person and teachings of Jesus Christ are not only within reach but also the source of a rich and sustainable life. In their low-key witness, there is a quiet power. The *hidden glory* of the vine and the branches is *manifested* in a way that embraces us all with the hope that we, also, are the blessed. "Blessed are those who hunger and thirst for righteousness, for they shall be satisfied" when the Lord comes again in "the glory of his righteousness and wonders of his love."

9

The Mountain

The arc of the Epiphany season comes to its close with a reading of the transfiguration narrative on the Sunday next before Lent. There have been changes in the lectionary in recent decades, not welcomed everywhere, particularly since there has long been a Feast of the Transfiguration already appointed for August 6.[1] However, it cannot be denied that it makes a most suitable observance at the climax of the season following the Feast of the Epiphany—for until the resurrection, there will be no greater manifestation of Jesus' unique divine glory than this one.[2]

On an unnamed mountaintop, Jesus appears in light so dazzling and unearthly that his garments shone whiter than any white known on earth (Mark 9:3).[3] Many attempts to explain the glory of God have been grounded in the idea of uncreated light.[4] This important theological concept about God's being can help us understand the biblical epiphanies. A vital text is Genesis 1:3—God is the sole giver of light, which appears at his mere word of command: "And God said, 'Let there be light'; *and there was light*"—just like that. God spoke light into existence. This is not the original light of his very self, however. It is second-order light that humankind is enabled to see. The light that belongs to God's self is *uncreated*, because it *precedes* creation. This distinction is important, because it preserves God's aseity (Latin *aseitas*, "being from itself"[5])—a central idea in the Christian tradition about God. That is, it preserves the essential distinction between God's *own being* and God's *revelation* of himself. John 1:3 ("without him was not anything made that was made"; see also John 1:10) and Hebrews 1:2 establish the Son with language that undergirds the doctrine of Jesus as the second person of the Trinity. He is not only *present* but *acting* at the creation.

There are important distinctions here. The glory of God is not God in himself. Human beings in our present sinful and limited condition are not able to see God directly.[6] God's glory is the radiance emanating *from* him. The light that *belongs* to him has to be mediated to us.

That is why, even in the least distanced descriptions of the divine *chabod* in the Old Testament, it is still an "appearance"—one step removed from its essence. It is "the *appearance of* the glory" that is shown on Mount Sinai (Exodus 24:17) rather than the glory itself. Likewise, when Moses asks to see God's glory (Exodus 33:18-23), he is only able to see God's "back"—the sight of God's face is forbidden. As we have already seen, the theophany vouchsafed to Ezekiel is even more distanced: "Such was the *appearance of* the *likeness of* the *glory of* the Lord" (Ezekiel 1:28). The effect of such passages serves as a warning to mere creatures that God's essence is not accessible but must be mediated so that human beings can receive it. Thus, when the glory of God appeared to the Israelites in the wilderness near Sinai, it was in a cloud (Exodus 16:10).[7]

Wonder of all wonders, this strongly emphasized Old Testament theme, "No one has ever seen God" (John 1:18), is precisely the grounding for the fourth evangelist's declaration that an ultimate *epiphaneia* has taken place. Because "the Word became flesh and dwelt among us," everything has changed. Now, "we have beheld his glory, glory as of the only Son from the Father" (John 1:14). As

Jesus himself will say a few chapters later, "He who sees me sees him who sent me" (John 12:45).

A crucial moment occurs in John 12, when some Gentiles visiting Jerusalem come up to the disciple Philip and boldly say, "Sir, we would see Jesus" (John 12:21 KJV).[8] This is the turning point in the Fourth Gospel, and many interpreters have linked John's special use of the *doxa* motif to the story of the transfiguration. When Jesus is told that Gentiles have come to him, he says, "The hour has come for the Son of man to be glorified" (John 12:23).

> "Now is my soul troubled. And what shall I say? 'Father, save me from this hour'? No, for this purpose I have come to this hour. Father, glorify thy name." Then a voice came from heaven, "I have glorified it, and I will glorify it again." The crowd standing by heard it and said that it had thundered. Others said, "An angel has spoken to him." Jesus answered, "This voice has come for your sake, not for mine. Now is the judgment of this world, now shall the ruler of this world be cast out; and I, when I am lifted up from the earth, will draw all men to myself." He said this to show by what death he was to die. The crowd answered him, "We have heard from the law that the

Christ remains for ever. How can you say that the Son of man must be lifted up? Who is this Son of man?" Jesus said to them, "The light is with you for a little longer. Walk while you have the light, lest the darkness overtake you; he who walks in the darkness does not know where he goes. While you have the light, believe in the light, that you may become sons of light." (John 12:27-36)

This luminous passage, which contains the motifs both of *showing* glory and *hiding* glory, gives powerful testimony to the identity of Father and Son and their sovereign freedom over their glory—when it is given and when it is hidden. What is not in doubt is the extraordinary claim that is being made. Jesus is the light of the world. When his light is hidden, the glory of God recedes into confounding darkness. (Yet, as we've already noted, the disappearance of the manifested *glory* does not mean the disappearance of God's *self*.)

This is the turning point of John's Gospel, as Jesus turns his face away from the scenes of his numerous "signs" toward the ultimate sign to take place in Jerusalem.[9] This means the ultimate contest with "the ruler of this world" and Jesus' apparent defeat. The glory manifested in the epiphanies we've seen during the season will seem to be extinguished at Golgotha. The fourth evangelist, by locating his special emphasis on the glorification of Jesus precisely at the turning point of his Gospel, signifies the relationship of that glorification to the crucifixion soon to come: "'Now shall the ruler of this world be cast out; and I, when I am lifted up from the earth, will draw all men to myself.' He said this to show by what death he was to die" (John 12:31-33).

Those who listen to a reading of the transfiguration narrative on the Sunday before the beginning of Lent will respond to the way it is presented. Conscientious readers of Scripture will submit themselves to the passage as its servants, not "acting it out," but offering it as those who are themselves addressed by it. The reader should pray to be enabled to convey the sense of wonder and awe that the evangelists intend. When the person preaching on that day is similarly struck by the force of what is being manifested in these events, there will be transfiguration of Christian believers. Those who are appointed to read aloud from the Scriptures in worship need to be apprised of the effect that their reading is meant to have. All too many untrained people go through their paces as if they were unaware of the glory of what they are reading. On rare occasions I have heard readings where the text seems to escape from the page with transforming power, but this only happens when readers subject themselves not to their own facility or talent, but to the power of the living Word of the living God.[10]

It became common, in the shift of emphasis in the mainline churches after the upheavals of the late sixties and beyond, to preach about the transfiguration in a remarkably tone-deaf way. Instead of focusing on Jesus' appearance in uncreated light and the voice of God the Father glorifying him, the preacher will pass quickly over the Moses and Elijah appearances and change the subject, going on, sometimes at length, about Peter's wish to stay in place on the mountain, thereby turning the story into an exhortation to the people in the pews to stop looking for mountaintop experiences and get down into the valley of hard knocks. Such interpretations ignore the carefully crafted passages in the Synoptics. An overview of the parallels is instructive; all three emphasize that the disciples "fell on their faces" (Matthew 17:6), that they were "exceedingly afraid" (Mark 9:6), and that "they were afraid as they entered the cloud" (Luke 9:34). Without this holy fear, the scene loses its power and there is nothing to lift the hearers into a dimension where they might experience the manifestation of the glory of the Lord.

The transfiguration scene is given great emphasis in all three Synoptics and appears in a Johannine form at the crucial turning point in the Fourth Gospel. It can serve as a summation of all that we have been saying about the glory of Jesus Christ during his earthly life as he approaches his Passion. As we look ahead to the final chapter in this book, a brief reflection on the relationship of the transfiguration and the Sermon on the Mount to the Christology of the Gospel of Matthew is in order.

It is clear throughout all the Gospels that Jesus' primary intention in gathering, teaching, and sending his disciples is that they are to carry not only the message of his kingdom but also—the feature of the gospel message that makes all else possible—*his living presence* among all who put their trust in him. The scene of the Great Commission at the conclusion of Matthew's Gospel is the most familiar and packs the most punch (or should). Jesus is about to ascend into heaven. He assembles his disciples (some of them still doubting!) and says:

All authority in heaven and on earth has been given
to me. Go therefore and make disciples of all nations, baptizing them in the name of the Father and
of the Son and of the Holy Spirit, teaching them to
observe all that I have commanded you; and behold
[*idou*], I am with you always, to the close of the age.
(Matthew 28:18-20)[11]

Here is a summation of the two pillars of Matthew's
structure: the ultimate power and authority at Jesus'
command, and the centrality of what he taught. A high
Christology underlies Matthew's project of elevating the
Sermon on the Mount. Many people like to quote the
saying in Matthew 7:21—"Not everyone who says to me,
'Lord, Lord,' shall enter the kingdom of heaven, but he
who does the will of my Father who is in heaven." It's
interesting that this is such a popular saying. Often it
comes off as a bit self-congratulatory! Here again,
though, Matthew and Paul are—in a sense—talking to
one another. Paul writes, "Work out your own salvation
with fear and trembling" (Philippians 2:12), another
very popular sentence—but an incomplete one! Paul
memorably follows this seemingly stern dictum with an
astonishing promise. As if in dialogue with Matthew,

Paul writes that the one who does the will of the Father is empowered by faith precisely in that one who "is at work in you, both to will and to work for his good pleasure" (Philippians 2:13). Notice the *empowering* effect of Paul's message. When we know that we *participate* in God's forward-moving purposes, already effective in us, that is truly to know transfiguration at work in the everyday.

Therefore, members of Christian communities need to be continually reminded that the transfiguration and the Sermon on the Mount are both equally part of the gospel message. Everything depends on who Jesus is. The person who is speaking in the sermon is the one who is able to give power to do the will of the Father. That is the *telos* (the purposed consummation) of Matthew's Gospel in the Great Commission toward which the Epiphany season moves. The new human being described in the Beatitudes is the one who has been brought into the presence of the transfigured and risen Lord, to whom "all authority in heaven and on earth" is given. The transfiguration of human nature depicted in the Sermon on the Mount is not achieved by human means. It is the gift of God, whose voice from the "radiant cloud" (*nephele photeine*—Matthew 17:5) identifies his Son, and it is the trajectory of the "therefore" in Romans 12:1-2 (NRSV):

> I appeal to you *therefore*, brothers and sisters, by the mercies of God, to present your bodies as a living sacrifice, holy and acceptable to God, which is your spiritual worship. Do not be conformed to this world, but be transformed [*transfigured*] by the renewing of your minds, so that you may discern what is the will of God—what is good and acceptable and perfect.

This is the glory of the Epiphany season, and a charge to preachers and teachers of the Christian faith. Telling stories about Jesus, what he said and what he did, is an essential part of spreading the gospel. But without the *doxa*, the glory as of the only Son from the Father, it is an incomplete gospel.

This is not only a summons to preachers and teachers but also to members of congregations. Those who listen to sermons and teachings can demand more than they are getting. "Sir, we would see Jesus." Congregations can remind their preachers and teachers that this what they are called to do: *to help us to see Jesus*—to pray and work

and speak always with the goal to help others to see him—
to see "the glory as of the only Son of the Father." The
author of the second letter of Peter makes a striking
appeal to Christians then and now, this very hour:

> For we did not follow cleverly devised myths when
> we made known to you the power and coming of
> our Lord Jesus Christ, but we were eyewitnesses of
> his majesty. For when he received honor and glory
> from God the Father and the voice was borne to
> him from the Majestic Glory, "This is My beloved
> Son, with whom I am well pleased," we heard this
> voice borne from heaven, for we were with him on
> the holy mountain. (2 Peter 1:16-18)

Sharing Peter's urgency that we should know the power
and the glory of our Lord, we conclude this climactic chapter
by focusing on the transfiguration as a gift bestowed upon
us by him. The Episcopal hymnal contains a striking translation of a fifteenth-century Latin hymn. Notice the emphasis on the purpose of God in Jesus Christ, who, in the
radiance of his majesty, "deigns to manifest" his glory as a
promise to his followers, who will be brought with him into

the joy of the perfect love that the Father shares with the Son. As members of his body, this is our ultimate destination.

> O wondrous type! O vision fair
> of glory that the Church may share,
> Which Christ upon the mountain shows,
> where brighter than the sun He glows! . . .
> With shining face and bright array,
> Christ deigns to manifest today
> What glory shall be theirs above
> who joy in God with perfect love.[12]

10

The Mission

Now the eleven disciples went to Galilee, to the mountain
to which Jesus had directed them. And when they saw him
they worshiped him; but some doubted. And Jesus came and
said to them, "All authority in heaven and on earth has been
given to me. Go therefore and make disciples of all nations,
baptizing them in the name of the Father and of the Son and
of the Holy Spirit, teaching them to observe all that
I have commanded you; and lo, I am with you always,
to the close of the age."

MATTHEW 28:16-20

Almighty God, whose Son our Savior Jesus Christ is the light of
the world: Grant that your people, illumined by your Word and
Sacraments, may shine with the radiance of Christ's glory, that
he may be known, worshiped, and obeyed to the ends of the earth;
through Jesus Christ our Lord, who with you and the Holy Spirit
lives and reigns, one God, now and for ever. Amen.

COLLECT FOR THE SECOND SUNDAY AFTER
THE EPIPHANY, BOOK OF COMMON PRAYER

In the nineteenth and twentieth centuries, until the upheavals of the late sixties and beyond, the season of Epiphany in the Episcopal Church was focused on mission. Children like me were instructed in Sunday school that the sheaves of wheat on the green altar hangings represented the growth of the gospel around the world.[1] This was strongly urged upon Episcopalians in those days. Collections were taken up for overseas missions, and prayers were offered for missionaries.

Unfortunately, this appears to have fallen out of fashion in the mainlines, probably because of today's greatly increased awareness of grievous harm done to other cultures by overzealous and misdirected missionaries. And yet some of the most heroic work in the world today is still done by Christian groups, as award-winning columnist Nicholas Kristof has repeatedly (and unfashionably) urged in the pages of *The New York Times*. Shame about what missionaries have done to indigenous cultures is imperative, and reparations are important, but the preaching of the gospel of Jesus Christ must never take a back seat.[2] The message of the living Lord Jesus was what drove the apostles to preach or die—often both—and God used that missionary preaching to spread the gospel around the world.

Those images of wheat remind us of the Word sown as seeds, to be reaped at harvest time. Thus, the Epiphany season has its own end-time dimension. The sheaf of wheat is not only a symbol of growth through mission but also a reminder of the great threshing floor on the last day. A hymn by Henry Alford is associated with Thanksgiving Day, but its imagery of harvest with its "fruitful ears" (that's you, readers) is that of the age to come:

> For the Lord our God shall come,
> and shall take his harvest home;
> from his field shall in that day
> all offenses purge away;
> giving angels charge at last
> in the fire the tares to cast,
> but the fruitful ears to store
> in his garner evermore.[3]

The purpose of Christian mission is to teach and preach the news of Jesus Christ, the Son of God who in his immolation takes the sin of the world (the "tares," or chaff) upon himself, and is gathering up all the works of the devil to be vanquished in his resurrection and second coming. If there is a hint of universal salvation here, so be it; it is only a hint, but the New Testament as a whole shows plainly that there is no one free from sin—all of us are "chaff" in a sense, for "none is righteous, no, not one" (Romans 3:10), and yet "as in Adam all die, even so in Christ shall all be made alive" (1 Corinthians 15:22). There has never been a message like this, and there has never been a redeemer like the Lord Jesus Christ in his glory.

This incomparable message has become diluted in various ways. This is a broad generalization and certainly does not apply in all cases, but in general there has been a trend in two more or less opposing directions. The left-leaning, "progressive" churches have tended to present Jesus as a great religious figure worthy of emulation, but not as John the Baptist identified him: the unique Lamb of God who takes away the sin of the world—let alone as the one who comes (*ho erchomenos*; see Revelation 1:4) on the last day to be our judge. The progressive churches typically think of sin as corporate, epitomized in prayers of repentance for such things as racism and poisoning the planet. These are indeed great evils. The problem, however, is that when everyone is responsible, no one is responsible— except zealots, and they annoy everyone else. (Again, this is a generalization, but not without basis.) The right-leaning, self-identified "evangelical" churches, on the other hand, tend to a highly individualized concept of sin and salvation with emphasis on a personal relationship with Jesus, which, in practice, can turn out to have little or no relation to anything in the Sermon on the Mount at the heart of Jesus' teaching.

The season of Epiphany, if its narrative structure is unfolded with the idea of glorifying Christ, is a powerful antidote to these unbalanced versions of the Christian message. In the chapter on the Sermon on the Mount in this book, we have seen that it lies at the heart of the gospel when it is understood as a description of a liberated life rather than a prescription for earning righteousness. Again: the "righteousness of God" (or "justice" of God—same word in Greek and Hebrew) is a gift and cannot be earned. If it is not understood as a gracious gift, it will lead to self-righteousness and division. When it is gratefully received as being undeserved and unearned, it is the ultimate good news for everyone. When this gospel message is withheld, in order to deliver some other message of self-creation, the church has indeed abandoned its reason for being.

Delivering the gospel message is the same thing as delivering the person of Jesus himself. Jesus is not a dead preacher. He is not an admirable person remote in time and difficult to emulate. He is alive and present in the power of the Holy Spirit. He is the hope of the whole world and of all its cultures and of each person in it. In him is the goodness, mercy, and grace of God for humanity— but more, in him is divine creative power. In the wedding feast at Cana we see his power over the natural world that produces grapes and wine at his mere word of command. In his calling of his disciples, we see how that same word of command calls forth an irresistible response from those he chooses. In his exorcisms, healings, and miracles, we see his powers over the forces of evil and his unique capacity to create new life even in people who might otherwise have resisted him.[4] The proclamation of the good news of the mission of Jesus is the foundation of the mission of the church. What an incomparable privilege this is, to bring the Word of life to "the nations"—to all the peoples of the earth.

The Epiphany season, when it is expounded and illuminated with gospel fervor, is uniquely suited to bridge the chasms in the life of the worldwide church. It presents

Jesus in all his divine splendor and command, while at the same time displaying the countless facets of his interactions with individual people. It shows his relationship with the Father. It reveals him confronting powers and principalities, and it shows him in intimate fellowship with those he befriends. It takes us through various episodes during his life when he became manifest (*epiphaneia*) in his glory, and at the same time in his humility. The season teaches us to value the entire fellowship of believers, because Jesus calls persons to himself without regard to their station, reputation, accreditation, or accomplishments—and we see how we can begin to be transformed by the action of his Holy Spirit working through the unearned and undeserved gifts that he bestows. The season with its readings takes us through some of the highest epiphanies in the life and mission of Jesus, from the adoration of the Magi to the transfiguration, leaving us well prepared for the beginning of the Passion narrative on Ash Wednesday.[5] "What child is this?" we sing at Christmastide. The season of Epiphany opens up the answer.

A Swedish pastor, Inger Rosdahl, has become a faithful friend on Twitter. She posted a simple yet powerful phrase: "our good and beautiful Lord Jesus." Yes, Jesus is beautiful: he is "Fairest Lord Jesus." In him is contained all of the wonder of creation—for as the second person of the Trinity, he is the sum and substance of the Maker of the original creation that was, the fallen creation that we now inhabit, and the perfected creation that is to come.

> For of him, and through him, and to him, are all things: to whom be glory for ever and ever. Amen. (Romans 11:36 KJV)

Coda: Doxology

In his penetrating book *The End of the Christian Life*, Todd Billings—who is living with incurable cancer—writes:

> One of my favorite parts of Sunday worship comes when I stand with the congregation and sing the Doxology. When young and old raise their voices together, the song becomes more than simply about us or our own lofty plans or even our own faith. When we sing, we sing a truth about reality, the central truth of the cosmos—a truth that endures whether we confess it or not, whether we are alive or not, whether any humans join the angels in singing it or not. The Doxology adores the one God who endures.[1]

The vocation of God's people, now and forever, is to praise the glory that God possesses, displays, and bestows upon creation and upon his gathered people. The calling of church leaders to design worship for *doxology* is a sacred and solemn one. This small book about the Feast of the Epiphany and its following season will have served its purpose if it encourages Christians to think more about the centrality of vibrant worship— the ascribing of ultimate worth, power, majesty, and glory to Jesus Christ—and in so doing, to be taken up into "the glories of his righteousness, and wonders of his love."

When we praise the glory of God, something of that glory is imparted to us. This is wonderful to understand and even more wonderful to experience. When we give glory to God, we are taken up into it. This can actually be felt by a worshiping congregation at times, when the preaching of the gospel evokes a sense of Christ's living presence and power, and the congregation feels itself lifted up.

Todd Billings touches on a central truth of the gospel here that should encourage us in this era of diminishing church attendance. The glory of God is not dependent upon us. He has graciously revealed it to us in Jesus, but we should not imagine that he is diminished if we are small in numbers. His faithfulness to his purposes for his creation will go forward no matter what size individual congregations might be.

God is not *dependent upon* us, but—amazing as it may seem—he *rejoices in* us. Part of God's purpose is that those who praise him, especially in common worship, will share the joy and the love of the blessed Trinity. When Black Christians emerge from their services, they will often say, "We had *church* today!" That can be taken to mean that there was a lot of rejoicing, but it also means more than that. It means that there was an enveloping sense of the living presence of the Lord in three Persons who empowers it all. Worship is "a sacrifice of praise" offered through Jesus by the Spirit, who actually causes our praise to bear fruit in spite of ourselves (Hebrews 13:15). In such worship we come to learn that this operation of the Spirit is like seed growing secretly, hidden from human sight until the Lord chooses to disclose it (Mark 4:26-29). Years after one Christian witness makes a simple confession about life in Jesus to a seeker, that recipient may in turn bear witness to that tiny seed, imparting its hidden growth into a lifegiving connection to the one true, everlasting Vine.

We never praise God in isolation, no matter how small the congregation, for we are accompanied by "the angels and archangels and all the company of heaven" (Book of Common Prayer)—the prophets and apostles, the martyrs and saints, and "the holy church throughout all the world," as in the words of the ancient canticle *Te Deum Laudamus.* The service of Holy Communion features the anthem *Gloria in Excelsis*, which begins "Glory be to God on high" and ends, "You alone, O Christ, with the Holy Spirit, are most high in the glory of God the Father." To recognize this, to attest to God's supreme glory is to be "lost in wonder, love, and praise." This is the true meaning of worship. From time to time, we humans will recognize that we and our doings, of which we are so vain, find their ultimate destiny—both for judgment and for redemption—in the overwhelming reality and power of the living God.

An abiding concern in ancient Israel was that the glory of Yahweh would be upheld over against the gods of the nations. Such gods are actually non-gods, without agency or existence, and worthy only of mockery.[2] Therefore, a chief component of doxology is the dethroning and devaluing of all idols that we put in God's place. The book of Revelation, which is one long doxology, summons the Christians under persecution to give glory to God above all else as their defense in the time of trial. Revelation contains more references to glory than any other book of the Bible, except the ever-important Psalms. The vision of the seer on the Isle of Patmos is the most comprehensive, sustained reflection on the "blessing and honor and *glory* and might" (Revelation 5:13) of God in Jesus Christ that is given to the church. The Scriptures are rounded out and completed by this final book, which is entirely devoted to the unfolding of the vision of the church in its ultimate identity as a kingdom of praise:

> After this I looked, and behold, a great multitude which no man could number, from every nation, from all tribes and peoples and tongues, . . . crying out with a loud voice, "Salvation belongs to our God who sits upon the throne, and to the Lamb! . . . Blessing and glory and wisdom and thanksgiving and honor and power and might be to our God for ever and ever! Amen." (Revelation 7:9-12)

The "ascriptions" in 1 Chronicles were commonly used in many Episcopal churches for many years, although the practice seems to have fallen out of fashion.[3] Many clergy in the mid-twentieth century were trained

to end their sermons by turning to the altar and reciting
this passage, which superbly evokes the surpassing
glories of God:

> Thine, O Lord, is the greatness, and the power, and
> the glory, and the victory, and the majesty; for all
> that is in the heavens and in the earth is thine; thine
> is the kingdom, O Lord, and thou art exalted as
> head above all. (1 Chronicles 29:11)[4]

And this ascription has frequently been used to summon
the people to make offerings as a way of praising
God's glory:

> Ascribe to the Lord the glory due his name;
>   bring an offering, and come before him!
>   (Psalm 96:8)

These liturgical praises are the proper response of
God's people to his being and attributes, but doubly so,
because the divine glory is not only his own unique pos-
session, but also his gift and blessing bestowed upon
those who worship him. It can't be said too often: the
wonder of this double meaning is that praising God (ascribing glory to him) is not only *something done* but also,
in the doing, something received:

Deliver us, O God of our salvation,

   and gather and save us from among the nations,

that we may give thanks to thy holy name,

   and *glory* in thy praise. (1 Chronicles 16:35)

Those charged with the responsibility of designing and leading worship in the churches of today will be encouraged by aiming at this purpose above all: that the people should experience God's supreme worth whenever they gather, whether for a simple morning prayer during Ordinary Time or an all-stops-out festival service. God's glory is not manifested only in splendor and trappings; more often, the prayer of a single penitent shows forth Christ's glory more truly than all the golden treasures accumulated over centuries in the worldwide church. Indeed, the very goal of the repentance for sin is not only personal deliverance for individual sinners one by one, but even more, it is dedicated to the glorification of God who delivers the entire fallen world through his Son.

The season of Epiphany is designed for the purpose of doxology. During the Sundays after the feast of January 6, a remarkable series of events in Jesus' earthly life, ministry, and teaching is unfolded precisely to reveal his glory in various ways, even as we move toward his destiny on the cross. The progression of Epiphany toward Lent and Holy Week shows that the cross of Christ *is* his glory, and the two ideas are inseparably held together in the New Testament. This gospel, this *evangel*, can never be allowed to grow stale. It must be retold "new every morning" in order that God's people may praise him without ceasing.

Therefore it is the heavenly calling of preachers, teachers, evangelists, and all other witnesses in this present time to declare the glory of Christ. The season after Epiphany is designed to do just this: to build up "from glory to glory" to the narrative of Jesus' Passion, crucifixion, and resurrection—the "hour of glory" around which the entire Fourth Gospel is shaped.

Reflecting upon the Words of Todd Billings

As I approach the midpoint of my ninth decade, I am passionately grateful to be alive, but at the same time acutely aware that the end is not far around the corner. Each day brings reminders of mortality. On a brilliant May morning I walk through a neighborhood bursting with flowers and blooming shrubs. I have an intense experience of rejoicing in the splendor of springtime, but at the same time I recognize that it will pass. Then it occurs to me that even the earth as we know it, in extremis as it is with our greed and folly, will also pass when God's new creation comes down from heaven. The apocalyptic passages of the New Testament envision this passing as cosmic rebirth, given by the hand of God. No one has understood this better than those who sang the African American spiritual:

> My Lord, what a morning
> When the stars begin to fall
> You'll hear the trumpet sound
> To wake the nations underground
>
> Looking to my God's right hand
> When the stars begin to fall
> You'll hear the sinner moan
> To wake the nations underground
> Looking to my God's right hand
>
> When the stars begin to fall
> You'll hear the Christian shout
> To wake the nations underground
> Looking to my God's right hand
> When the stars begin to fall.

This summons to praise God's releases us from all our earthly burdens and fears of the future as we honor the

Creator—not just by rejoicing in creation in its present damaged state, but also by enlisting in the Lord's work of rescuing his handiwork. May we pray and work ceaselessly to join in *his* mighty work of redemption, that our heedless rapacity may not be the last word for our planet, but an enemy vanquished, never to rise again.

Doxology—rejoicing in the Lord and praising the glory of Christ in the fellowship of the saints—is the one great offering that will be the same in this world and the next. As we are momentarily taken up out of ourselves in this world, how much more shall we all together be taken up into the dance of the blessed Three in One for ever and ever.

Gloria in excelsis Deo!

Notes

Author's Preface

[1] From the Collect for Advent II, Book of Common Prayer.

[2] In the 1979 Book of Common Prayer, the Proper Preface is different: " . . . because in the mystery of the Word made flesh, you have caused a new light to shine in our hearts, to give the knowledge of your glory in the face of your son Jesus Christ our Lord." There is nothing wrong with this; after all, it's 2 Corinthians 4:6! But the earlier version contains the promise that we will be brought "out of darkness into his own glorious light."

Introduction

[1] There were three traditional designations for the Great Church: the Church Militant, the Church Expectant, and the Church Triumphant. We used to hear a lot about this in the fifties, though not so much today. It would be profitable to rethink what it means to be the Church Militant in a nuclear age. See the chapter on the Sermon on the Mount below.

[2] It can properly be argued that Epiphany is a feast day, not a "season." The Sundays after the Epiphany are called just that in the lectionary and in the Book of Common Prayer. For theological, homiletical, and evangelistic purposes, however, I think the Sundays following the feast day, with their narrative sequence inherited from the earliest centuries, can very well be called a season.

[3] Because of the quite drastic difference from year to year in the number of Sundays in the Epiphany season, preachers and worship leaders must be particularly intentional about shaping the season for proclamation.

[4] It is encouraging to note that major work has been done in recent decades to reclaim Advent as the season of the last things, rather than just "preparation for Christmas," a most unfortunate designation that left the season virtually defenseless against being swallowed whole by commercial Christmas.

[5] The rise of the Pentecostal denominations in the twentieth century has helped people understand something of the Holy Spirit as a living third person of the Trinity. The Pentecost volume in this series, by Emilio Alvarez, will be very beneficial in this regard.

[6] This hymn is by Christopher Wordsworth, who was the nephew of William Wordsworth, the great English Lake District poet. Christopher Wordsworth was a prominent cleric in the Church of England who rose to become bishop of Lincoln. He is buried in Lincoln Cathedral.

[7] It is amusing to note that the Episcopal hymnal has changed the words "God in flesh" to "God in man." This is ironic, in view of all the contortions to get rid of the generic "man" in the liturgy! In church music, there has been an almost wholesale flight from the language of previous centuries. This is a major loss to the church. I admit that "leddest" shows Bland Tucker in a rare weak moment, but it is unfortunate that young people are not more at ease with earlier literary styles. It has been shown that churchgoers who grew up with the older rites of Common Prayer find it easier to read Shakespeare (not to mention John Donne and a host of others).

[8] This can be powerfully illustrated by a key moment in the life of Martin Luther King Jr. During a visit to Montgomery, Alabama, I visited the Civil Rights Museum there. One of the exhibits, a diorama, showed King sitting alone at his kitchen table in the middle of the night. The teenaged guide intoned solemnly, "This is the epiphany." I am not sure she knew what the word meant; it was a phrase she had been taught to say. No one asked for a further explanation. The diorama depicted a major turning point in the life of Dr. King that has indeed been called "the kitchen epiphany." The episode has been described in various biographies, the source being King himself. He told how, at a low point in his crusade when he was under attack from many directions, he sat alone in the dark kitchen and considered giving up. He then heard the voice of Jesus saying, "I will never, never leave you alone." That "manifestation" was not summoned up by him; it was *given* to him to strengthen him for the long and perilous road ahead.

[9] This has entered the common sphere. See for instance Charles Marsh's mesmerizing book *God's Long Summer* (Princeton, NJ: Princeton University Press, 1997).

1. THE GLORY

[1] We might wish that this name for the day and season had stuck, because it makes the meaning of *manifestation* even more potent: Epiphany is not just a showing of a generically spiritual nature, but a showing specifically of *the three-personed God*.

[2] The Greek word *doxa* is easy to remember if one knows the doxology of the church: "Glory be to God on high . . . ." Since *logos* means "word," *doxology* means "word of glory," or, more specifically, the words spoken by the church in praise of God in Christ. The Latin is also familiar: *Gloria in excelsis Deo.*

[3] As I was working on this book, I could not help reflecting on the sermons I've heard since I contracted to write it, a few months before the Covid pandemic. During the strange years that have followed the lockdown of 2020, I have heard (mostly online, but also in person) at least two hundred sermons from various churches, mostly but not all Episcopal. More often than not, I have been struck by the absence of any specific mention of the glory of God, specifically in Jesus Christ, which, I am arguing, is the theme of the Epiphany season—a theme that in fact adorns the entire biblical message. As I reflect on my own sermons over forty-seven years, I wonder if I should not have been more focused on the *doxa tou theou* (see John 11:40—at the tomb of Lazarus, Jesus says to Martha, "Did I not tell you that if you would believe you would see *the glory of God?*").

[4] The phrase "the appearance of" sets the glory of God at a remove from human perception. We will meet this again in Ezekiel.

[5] Abbot Suger of the cathedral of Saint Denis in Paris wished to show the glory of God in his sublime architectural designs. It was a noble wish. Not everyone who visits the great basilica is moved to reflect upon the glory of God, however. I went there to see the French kings' tombs and was unexpectedly bowled over by the breathtaking interior, but I can't honestly say that it led me to an epiphany of God in Jesus Christ.

[6] *Effulgence* is defined in Webster's revered second edition as "diffusing a flood of resplendent light." That's probably as close as we're likely to get to the Bible's definition of glory. It is clearly one step away from being God *in himself*. It is his diffused radiance, not his essence that we perceive, and even then we perceive it only when he grants it, not when we try to conjure it up. Not everyone discerned the glory of Jesus: "But to all who received him . . . he gave power to become children of God" (John 1:12).

[7] It should be repeatedly stressed: there is no discontinuity or disunity between Jesus Christ and the God of the Old Testament.

[8] John Bowring, "In the Cross of Christ I Glory," Hymnary.org, 1825, www.hymnary.org/text/in_the_cross_of_christ_i_glory_towering.

[9] "Glory," Wiktionary, February 25, 2023, www.en.wiktionary.org/wiki/glory; italics added. I am not recommending Wikipedia as a reliable academic source! But since it is so widely used, its definitions have influence.

[10] Walter Chalmers Smith, "Immortal, Invisible, God Only Wise," Hymnary.org, 1867, www.hymnary.org/text/immortal_invisible_god_only_wise.

[11] It is of great importance to note that Ezekiel prophesies in a foreign land where he and his people have experienced defeat and exile. The glory of the God of Israel is not diminished in alien, hostile territory.

[12] In the Bible there is no vision without audition. What Ezekiel *hears*—the Word of the Lord—is more important than what he *sees*. This should be a basic theological foundation for all Christian teaching.

[13] This astonishing verse has been expounded thousands of times. For me, it was the Rev. Jack Gilpin, an Episcopal priest and character actor well known to fans of stage and television, who enacted Ezekiel 1:28 in the most memorable way, emphasizing the three *of*s that so effectively remove the glory of God from the possibility of unaided human conception.

[14] At my father's funeral these words, "We shall be changed," were read so humbly, yet so prophetically, by one of the lay leaders of the congregation that it seemed as if he was himself being changed by the power of the Word of God even as he was reading it. He said to me afterward that he had studied the passage diligently because "I wanted to know what Saint Paul meant." That would be a good motto for anyone reading the Scripture for public worship.

[15] Karl Barth, *The Epistle to the Romans*, preface to the second edition. George Hunsinger expounds this succinctly in "The Infinite Qualitative Difference and the Difference It Makes: A Recurring Theme in Barth's Dogmatics," *University of Toronto Journal of Theology* 36, no. 2 (Fall 2020): 183-93.

[16] I have often heard members of the Black church exclaim, "God is able." In a sense, those three simple words say it all.

[17] We might say today, What is the chief and highest end [goal, purpose] of humanity?

[18] The Westminster Shorter Catechism goes on to edify:
Q. 2. What rule has God given to direct us how we may glorify and enjoy *him?*

A. The word of God, which is contained in the Scriptures of the Old and New Testaments, is the only rule to direct us how we may glorify and enjoy him.

[19] C. S. Lewis, "The Weight of Glory," in *The Weight of Glory and Other Addresses* (New York: HarperOne, 2001 [1949]), 42.

[20] *Eschaton* (Greek) means "last." *Eschatology* simply means "speaking of the last [day]"—the day of the Lord, the arrival of the kingdom, the second coming of the Lord.

[21] From the hymn "Alleluia, Sing to Jesus," originally from 2 Corinthians 3:18: "We all . . . are being changed into his likeness from one degree of glory to another."

[22] We will return to this phrase from Isaac Watts's "Joy to the World" more than once.

[23] I have modernized the spelling, e.g., "star" for "starre."

[24] Second Corinthians is actually more than one letter pieced together. Parts of it are painful to read, as Paul struggles to express his concern and dismay. However, it is full of supremely important passages.

[25] Nikolaus Decius, "All Glory Be to God on High," trans F. Bland Tucker, Hymnary.org, 1525, www.hymnary.org/hymn/EH1982/421; italics added.

2. THE DAY

[1] In studying the origins of Epiphany, we will refer to the Eastern Church and the Western church as they were before the Great Schism of 1054. The Eastern Church was centered in Constantinople and is known today as the Eastern Orthodox Church. The Western church was centered in Rome, but since the Reformation it has divided into multitudinous directions, splitting from the Roman Catholic Church into countless Protestant denominations and groups.

[2] Much ink has been spilled concerning the fixed date for Christmas, December 25. Many people today take it for granted that the church chose this date to celebrate the birth of Jesus because it coincides with the winter solstice—the return of the sun. Few nonspecialists are aware that this hypothesis (called *Sol Invictus* or History of Religions hypothesis) has been vigorously called into question by more recent scholarship, especially among Anglophones. The prominent scholar Thomas Talley strongly argued that there is little historical evidence for the "solar hypothesis," and that the date of Christmas was chosen in the third century AD because it was computed from the supposed date of Jesus' conception nine months before. This is called the "computation

hypothesis." This viewpoint is significant because, if true, it undermines the foundations of a syncretistic Christmas without Christ.

[3] A rich, colorful depiction of Epiphany customs was published in "Epiphany Celebrations Around the World," *The New York Times*, January 6, 2018, www.nytimes.com/2018/01/06/world/epiphany-christmas.html. Three years later, on January 6, 2021, the United States Capitol was stormed by a crowd of enraged demonstrators. On that day of infamy, there was no mention of the Feast of the Epiphany in the *Times*.

3. The Season

[1] J. Neil Alexander, *Celebrating Liturgical Time* (New York: Church Publishing, 2014), 37.

[2] Note 2 in the introduction addresses the problem of referring to Epiphany as a "season." Strictly speaking, the Sundays after Epiphany are not a "season" in the same sense as Advent, Lent, and Easter. However, the themes of the weeks following the feast day are so strongly ordered according to ancient practice that I believe they can very well be called a season.

[3] The tangled discussion concerning the dates of Christmas and Epiphany and the way in which their identities were shaped in the first five centuries is difficult for a nonspecialist to follow. I have pored over a number of sources, but the debate is daunting. I have chosen to simplify by stating the most basic, undisputed factors in the shaping of the feast day of January 6 and the season following, as witness to the manifestation of Jesus Christ's identity, mission, and glory.

[4] These basic facts about the development of the season are widely available in scholarly reference books. I have used Paul F. Bradshaw and Maxwell E. Johnson, *The Origins of Feasts, Fasts, and Seasons in Early Christianity* (Collegeville, MN: Liturgical Press, 2011); Thomas J. Talley, *The Origins of the Liturgical Year,* 2nd ed. (Collegeville, MN: Liturgical Press, 1986); and F. L. Cross and E. A. Livingstone, eds., *Oxford Dictionary of the Christian Church*, 3rd ed. (New York: Oxford University Press, 2005), among other works.

[5] Similarly, in the listing of the Collects in the Book of Common Prayer, we have Sundays "after Christmas Day" and "after Pentecost," because the days of those seasons follow a specific, singular feast day. In contrast, we have Sundays "of Advent," "in Lent," and "of Easter" (Eastertide has rightly become known as "The Great Fifty Days").

[6] The lectionary should never be the sole guide to Scripture, because it is selective, and the passages appear out of context. Moreover, there are a great many portions of the Bible that are not in the lectionary. The Bible should be studied, known, and loved *as a whole*—always with the witness of the First Testament without which the hope for a Messiah is rootless and malnourished. This small book would have been infinitely richer if we'd had space for the full 365-day lectionary, including especially the Psalms that testify to Christ (as, in a sense, they all do). Even this limited study, however, is useful as a teaching framework, because it is structured according to a way that the church has experienced, understood, and proclaimed the *epiphany* of Jesus Christ over two thousand years.

[7] Carl Turner, the rector of St. Thomas Fifth Avenue, relates how the renowned New Testament scholar C. K. Barrett habitually addressed his classes at the beginning of term by writing Jesus' question in Matthew 22 on the chalkboard, then turning to the students and telling them that this question would be at the center of all their studies.

4. THE STAR

[1] The Magi competed with the baptism of Jesus for center stage on January 6 for the first four centuries. It was in the fifth century that Pope Leo the Great definitively assigned the Magi to that date.

[2] "Balthasar, Melchior, and Gaspar" have been traditionally depicted as something approximating White, Brown, and Black, as can still be seen in any child's painted crèche today.

[3] We may surely enjoy and appreciate the delight that costume-making and pageantry has given to generations of children and adults. The opportunity for teaching, however, should not be ignored! Families who have crèche figures and wish to enact the Twelve Days of Christmas can enjoy moving the three Magi gradually from a distance across the house to get closer to the holy family in time for Three Kings Day on January 6.

[4] The scholarly consensus today is that Matthew's community was originally largely Jewish converts, in a major city—perhaps Antioch—but had become mostly Gentile by the time Matthew's Gospel was put together.

[5] This historical fact is also reflected in the Gospel and Epistles of John.

[6] Raymond E. Brown, *The Birth of the Messiah* (New York: Doubleday, 1993), 199. Brown's typically thorough examination of all the issues is a truly indispensable resource for everything concerning the infancy narratives in

the New Testament. Brown was one of my important teachers at Union Theological Seminary in New York; *The Birth of the Messiah* and *The Death of the Messiah* (New York: Doubleday, 1994) are his most useful books for preachers.

[7] This Herod is "Herod the Great," who built the Second Temple. The historical Herod was indeed a usurper of sorts. The Herod who condemned and crucified Jesus was his son Herod Antipas.

[8] This sixteenth-century "Coventry Carol" in a minor key is still sung by many choral groups. It originated from Coventry in England, where it was traditionally performed as a mystery play.

[9] This aspect of the story has come into greater prominence in recent years as the internet has enabled us to see desperate refugees as never before.

[10] The striking text of this Christmas carol, by Robert Southwell, Roman Catholic martyr, was set to music by Benjamin Britten in his much-loved *Ceremony of Carols*. Southwell was English by birth and upbringing, but was educated in Paris and Rome and returned to Protestant England as a clandestine missionary. He was arrested in England in 1592 on the charge of high treason against Elizabeth I, suffered unspeakable tortures under Elizabeth's infamous enforcer Richard Topcliffe, and died in an excruciating public execution in 1595 at Tyburn (Thomas More was spared by Elizabeth's father Henry VIII from this form of execution). Thus Southwell exalted the victory of Christ over evil and death in his own suffering.

[11] Charles Wesley, "Come, Thou Long-Expected Jesus," Hymnary.org, 1744, www.hymnary.org/text/come_thou_long_expected_jesus_born_to.

[12] Paul says this another way in Romans 11 when he speaks of the "grafting in" of the Gentiles (Romans 11:11-32) as the ultimate eschatological event. There can be no overstating the importance of this passage for Jewish-Christian relations. One may say that the Magi recast as kings represent that "grafting in" as they pay homage to the ultimate King of the Jews and Gentiles. There are many layers here.

[13] "The Song of Simeon," as it is called, is poetry; it is a canticle. *Nunc Dimittis* is Latin for "Now let depart." When I was a little girl growing up in Franklin, Virginia, our very small parish church always had Evening Prayer during Lent. In those days the "The Song of Simeon" canticle was never said at Morning Prayer. The only time you could hear it was at Evening Prayer. It is much more suitable for that hour. When I was a small child in the evening light at our church, the words of the *Nunc Dimittis* impressed themselves deeply upon me: "Lord, now lettest thou thy servant depart in peace,

according to thy word, for mine eyes have seen thy salvation." Now that I am eighty-five (Anna's age!), they mean much more. I can echo Simeon's words now with deep joy and conviction.

[14] Raymond E. Brown notes this repeatedly in *The Birth of the Messiah: A Commentary on the Infancy Narratives in the Gospels of Matthew and Luke,* The Anchor Yale Bible Reference Library (New York: Doubleday, 1993). Luke (and perhaps his sources) seems particularly intent upon anchoring the birth of Christ in the messianic traditions of Judaism.

5. THE RIVER

[1] Around the world, Epiphany traditions sometimes seem to have little to do with the feast itself. On January 6 in Eastern countries like Bulgaria and Russia, customs include a boisterous diving competition to rescue a wooden cross thrown into freezing lake water, with accompanying hilarity.

[2] The temptation in the wilderness is prominent in the season of Lent, so it will not be discussed here.

[3] Revelation concretely recognizes the eschatological identity of Jesus in this way: he is *ho erchomenos*, the one who is to come (Revelation 1:4). The Synoptic Gospels place the Baptizer at the intersection of the ages; he is the voice announced in Isaiah 40, not merely as "a voice crying in the wilderness" but as the one who heralds the coming collision of this present evil age (Galatians 1:4). The link between John the Baptist and the prophecy of Isaiah in 40:3-5 is quintessential biblical apocalyptic, of which Ernst Käsemann famously wrote, "Apocalyptic was the mother of all Christian theology," (*New Testament Questions of Today* [Minneapolis: Fortress, 1969], 102). It is debatable whether John is the last prophet of the old age or the first prophet of the age to come, but either way, he stands at the apocalyptic frontier where the collision is taking place, and we cannot overemphasize his importance as the herald of the arrival of the Messiah. His fate at the hands of the Herodian family prefigures the destiny of Jesus.

[4] Matthew 24, Mark 13, and Luke 21:5-36 constitute the remarkable, triple-tradition "Synoptic apocalypse." Ignored, even scorned, for many years by many interpreters, these chapters came back into favor after World War II.

[5] Isaiah 42:1-9 ("Behold my servant, whom I uphold, my chosen . . .") is always read on the first Sunday after the Epiphany. This passage has unfortunately become tame and predictable since the late sixties (in the same way as Luke 4:16-30, the sermon in the synagogue at Nazareth), with its messianic and eschatological dimensions largely suppressed.

[6] Jesus continues by saying that the least person in heaven is greater than John the Baptist. This is not to undercut the Baptizer but rather to heighten dramatically the break with hierarchies of the past that Jesus represents (In Romans 4:5, Paul makes the point differently by saying that in Jesus, God justifies the ungodly). In that sense, there is no "least person" in the kingdom of heaven!

[7] John the Baptist gets his full due (or should, if preachers are paying attention) in Advent, with two adjacent Sundays devoted to his apocalyptic preaching.

[8] Admittedly it is a challenge to preach in this way if infants are being baptized, but since godparents are asked to "renounce Satan and all the spiritual forces of wickedness" (Book of Common Prayer, 1979), the apocalyptic imagery is not entirely missing!

[9] Many Christians have been taught that there are three words for love in Greek, and they know that *agape* is the most important one (see 1 Corinthians 13). The fact that *righteousness* and *justice* are the *same word* in Hebrew and Greek should be equally well known and should shape the church's thinking about social ethics.

[10] Roman Catholic translations, in particular, tend to use "justice" to translate *dikaiosyne*. Perhaps this helped Catholic theologians to understand the theological connection between the gospel and social justice better than Protestants did in the twentieth and twenty-first centuries, as evidenced by the excellence of Catholic social teaching.

[11] Aloys Grillmeier, *Christ in Christian Tradition* (London: Sheed and Ward, 1965), 79-80.

[12] I come from a tradition of infant baptism, but there is much to be said for baptism by consent of the baptizand. The baptism (often by full immersion) of a preteen child or adult who has chosen to be baptized has a powerful effect.

[13] "Joy to the World," by the hymn-writer Isaac Watts (1674-1748), is a rendering of Psalm 98 and was never intended to be a Christmas hymn. Watts sought to bring liveliness and commitment to the singing of Psalms. When the lyrics of this hymn are read in a seasonally neutral context, it can clearly be seen that it is not about the nativity, but instead looks forward to the second coming when Christ will be recognized in all his glory as the judge of all the earth. The complementary Psalm 99 even more obviously connects justice and righteousness in v. 4. (In spite of the imagery of the second coming, "Joy to the World" is not really in the spirit of the Advent season

either, because it does not have the now-not yet tension of Advent. Ascension Day perhaps comes closest to the combination of justice and righteousness in an apocalyptic context. In any case, it will be obvious that "the glories of his righteousness" must be understood in the context of the Old Testament as well as the New.)

6. The Wine

[1] The word for "behold" (*idou*) is typically translated "see" today, presumably because "behold" is regarded as quaint. This is a great mistake. In biblical Hebrew and Greek, it is a striking, revelatory word. It does not mean "look!" or "see!" It means looking with new eyes upon a hitherto inaccessible reality now revealed by the will and purpose of God.

[2] It is a striking fact that in the patristic period, there were more commentaries written on the Song of Songs than any other biblical book except the Psalms. The book of Hosea also uses the image of marriage to convey the devotion of a faithful God to his wayward people. See especially Hosea 2:16-23.

[3] This paragraph in the 1979 Book of Common Prayer has similar wording, but the rolling cadence is gone.

[4] See also Amos 9:13; Joel 3:13; and Jeremiah 31:5.

[5] This is true of all the evangelists, including Luke the "historian," but it is more obvious in John because of his striking dramatic gifts. A "gospel" is a genre unique to the New Testament.

[6] Rudolf Bultmann, *The Gospel of John* (Louisville, KY: Westminster John Knox, 1971), 68.

[7] I once heard a literary critic, a militant atheist, criticize modern reinventions of the New Testament Jesus, whom he described as "a commanding figure." Sometimes an unbeliever can be rightly resistant to projecting sentimentality into the Bible.

[8] Most interpreters have long agreed that Jesus intends no disrespect to his mother. He does, however, put a certain distance between her and himself. There is no sentimentality about Mary in the New Testament. She acts here, as she does elsewhere in the Gospels, not as his mother, but as his disciple. She has no idea what he might do, but she has faith that he can and will do *something*. The striking aspect of his reply to her is the link between Jesus' "hour"—the hour in which the glory revealed in the miracle at Cana will be shown to be a strange glory indeed, the hour of his suffering and death. Thus the third major event of Epiphany—following the Magi's visit and the baptism of the Lord—links the season to Lent.

[9] Here is Calvin's tribute: "It is a high honor given to marriage, that Christ not only deigned to be present at a nuptial banquet, but honored it with his first miracle." John Calvin, *Commentary on the Gospel According to John*, trans. William Pringle (Grand Rapids, MI: Baker, 1984).

[10] Rudolf Schnackenburg, *The Gospel According to St. John*, vol. 1 (New York: Crossroad, 1982), 336, author's emphasis. Schnackenburg writes that the *doxa* of Jesus is primarily his divine and creative power (*dunamis*), which is proper to him as God. In John, the concept of *dunamis*, so important to Paul, is subsumed into his *doxa*. Therefore the "signs" (John's word) of *power* that he performs are manifestations (epiphanies) of his *glory* "as of the only Son from the Father" (John 1:14).

7. THE MINISTRY

[1] The confrontation with Satan is front and center in John's Gospel also, but— as is typical with John—it is expressed in a different way: "Now is the judgment of this world, now shall the ruler of this world be cast out" (John 12:31).

[2] The temptation and Gethsemane properly belong to Lent. I mention them here to show how crucial the struggle with the adversary is for understanding Jesus' glory as the one who has ultimate power over the demonic realm.

[3] Many scholars who understand Paul capitalize Sin and Death to emphasize their status as great powers.

[4] It must be admitted that the selections about Jesus' earthly ministry are somewhat sparse in the Epiphany lectionary. That, however, is because it is a short season. It is also because much space is (quite rightly) given to the Sermon on the Mount (in year A) and its Lukan version called the Sermon on the Plain (in year C). The point is that the lectionary choices for the season strongly demonstrate the unified purpose of the evangelists and apostles. They are not just giving us stories about a spiritual celebrity who did remarkable deeds and taught remarkable things. Each of them seeks to display him unequivocally as the anointed Son of God and Messiah of Israel. Since Epiphany is such a short season, preachers and teachers should embrace the opportunity on Sundays during the lengthy season of Ordinary Time to continue the theme of *epiphaneia*, since all of the New Testament (and much of the Old, seen through New Testament eyes) manifests Jesus' glory in one way or another. Without these epiphanies, there is no gospel.

8. The Teaching

[1] Epiphany is a short season in view of all that it tries to do, and in some years, when Easter Day is early, it is *really* short. Therefore, although the Sermon on the Mount (in year A) and the Sermon on the Plain (in year C) are clearly highlighted, the selections are incomplete. It is therefore important to schedule opportunities for preaching, teaching, and studying the entire Sermon on the Mount at other times of the year—perhaps in Ordinary Time. The Bruderhof offers an excellent guide for group study in *Following the Call: Living the Sermon on the Mount Together,* ed. Charles E. Moore (Walden, NY: Plough Publishing House, 2021). The word *Together* in the subtitle makes all the difference. It is of utmost significance that the sermon is not meant to be an ethic for solitary individuals.

[2] This has never been stated with more depth and insight than in Abraham Lincoln's second inaugural address. See Ronald C. White Jr.'s dazzling analysis, *Lincoln's Greatest Speech* (New York: Simon & Schuster, 2002).

[3] Actually, the author of James almost certainly knew of Paul's preaching and was working in dialogue with it; otherwise, it would never have been in the canon. There it remains, despite Martin Luther's disdain for it ("an epistle of straw").

[4] The problem in many "progressive" congregations who are committed to works of justice and peace is that the works become ends in themselves, resulting in little true awareness of one's standing before God. The like-minded members of the congregation who are committed to the works are convinced of their righteousness, and the people who are not able or willing to be so committed feel resentful, estranged, and disabled. Preaching and teaching that gets the balance right will result in the enabling of *all* the faithful, with respect for those who may not have the same abilities or passions. Servants of justice and peace like Dietrich Bonhoeffer and Martin Luther King Jr. remain important and encouraging for everyone because they always kept this balance, aware that there will always be many who will not, or cannot, check all the boxes.

[5] Richard Lischer, "The Sermon on the Mount as Radical Pastoral Care," *Interpretation* 41, no. 2 (January 1987): 157-69. In preparation for writing this chapter, I consulted a good many books (the literature on the sermon is vast). Among them, I found Lischer's essay to be the most helpful for pastors and church leaders. For the purposes of this series on the church calendar, it is noteworthy that Lischer emphasizes the liturgy (Lutheran in

his case) as the fruitful source of learning how to live the life of the sermon communally. This is a very promising proposal, and not as far-fetched as one might think.

6 Lischer, "The Sermon on the Mount."

7 Lischer, "The Sermon on the Mount."

8 A publication at their hundredth anniversary, *Another Life Is Possible* (Walden, NY: Plough Publishing House, 2021), is a beautifully illustrated collection of testimonies by members of Bruderhof communities from America to Australia. Their quarterly publication, *Plough*, features short articles by a remarkably diverse assortment of nonmember supporters who share some of the Bruderhof's aspirations and commitments. Another book from Plough, *Following the Call,* ed. Moore, is a representative collection of reflections on the Sermon on the Mount from contributors ranging from John Chrysostom to Madeleine l'Engle. Over many decades, I have been the recipient of their relaxed way of sharing their vision with others, without a hint of pressure or judgment. Their witness is a living illustration to the rest of us that the Sermon on the Mount is not fantasy beyond reach.

9 Find them online at www.bruderhof.com and on Twitter @TheBruderhof.

10 Rowan Williams, the 104th Archbishop of Canterbury, is an admirer of the Bruderhof. He writes, "There is no sectarian aggression here—clear and uncompromising principle, yes, but not the urge to demean or despise others. My friends in the Bruderhof . . . trust the God of peace sufficiently to give their lives to incarnating the peace of God" (Foreword, *Another Life Is Possible*).

9. The Mountain

1 The day was also known as Quinquagesima Sunday, to denote the number of days till Easter Day (using a somewhat contorted method way of counting days). Octogenarian Episcopalians remember a "Pre-Lent" of three Sundays called Septuagesima, Sexagesima, and Quinquagesima. This usage is still in place in parts of the Church of England.

2 The Roman Catholic Church has maintained the tradition that the glory of Christ's person manifested in the transfiguration on a mountaintop antici- pates the eschaton.

3 Scripture does not name the mountain. Especially in Eastern Orthodoxy, it was thought to be Mount Tabor. In later tradition, many scholars have argued that the transfiguration passages are a post-resurrection scene

relocated to the ministry. As for John, it is a truism that the whole Fourth Gospel is a transfiguration!

4 The fourteenth-century Eastern Orthodox doctrine of uncreated light ("Tabor light") has certain interesting features that can help us to appreciate the pre-existence and sublime otherness—the *doxa*—of God. The light of the transfiguration on Mount Tabor and, by extension, the blinding light seen by the apostle Paul at his conversion were thought to be uncreated light. This light is a *manifestation* of God that is entirely in God's power to give and to withhold, and impossible to attain otherwise. The radical position taken in these pages is that no amount of spiritual practice or discipline can produce such visions, but only the pure gift of God, which comes unbidden and unearned. Biblical epiphanies are always surprises.

5 "'Aseity' . . . is the traditional divine attribute whereby God is said to exist of or from himself [Latin *a se*]. . . . God's lack of dependence on anything besides himself distinguishes him radically from creatures, every one of which depends on God, and therefore on at least one thing besides itself" (Walter Matthews Grant, "Aseity," Routledge Encyclopedia of Philosophy, 2015, www.rep.routledge.com/articles/thematic/aseity/v-1).

6 "Though the eye of sinful man thy glory may not see," from the hymn "Holy, Holy, Holy."

7 In Exodus 24:9-10 we read that the elders of Israel "saw the God of Israel," but in fact it was the sapphire pavement beneath his feet that was seen. It is said that Moses talked to God "face to face" (Exodus 33:11), but this can't be literal because nine verses later we read that "man shall not see me and live" (Exodus 33:20). At the end of Exodus we read that Moses was not able to enter the temple of meeting because "the glory of the Lord filled the tabernacle" (Exodus 40:35).

8 The church needs more lay people who will say to their preachers and teachers, "We want to see Jesus."

9 In *The Transfiguration of Politics* (New York: Harper & Row, 1975), Paul Lehmann powerfully calls upon the fourth evangelist's unique interpretation of Jesus' glory to make a theological link with Martin Luther King Jr.'s famed "I Have a Dream" speech. He notes that one of King's "otherwise gifted" biographers was blind to the way King quoted Isaiah and evoked the Day of the Lord, thereby failing to understand the power of Christian faith to interpret the signs of the times and prepare for "the great sufferings yet to be endured."

[10] Dietrich Bonhoeffer's instructions about reading Scripture in worship in *Life Together* are invaluable.

[11] *Idou* in the New Testament is a revelatory word pointing to another dimension. "Lo" is sometimes used to translate *idou,* but "behold" is stronger and better captures the transvisionary quality of the Greek. "Look" and "see" fail in this regard.

[12] "O Wondrous Type! O Vision Fair," trans. John Mason Neale from *Coelestis formam gloriae* (1495), Hymnary.org, 1861, www.hymnary.org/hymn /EH1982/136.

10. The Mission

[1] My attention to those sheaves of wheat was greatly heightened by the visit to our diocese of a dynamic Episcopal missionary priest who, in the 1940s and '50s, traveled around the parishes with slide shows and compelling stories of the church's overseas missions. I am sorry that I have been unable to remember or retrieve his name. To this day I associate the Epiphany season with the spread of the gospel message.

[2] Reaction against missionary work can be carried too far. Nelson Mandela is not the only colonized person who has been grateful to missionaries; he often spoke of his fondness for the Methodists who taught him as a child.

[3] Henry Alford, "Come, Ye Thankful People, Come," Hymnary.org, 1844, www.hymnary.org/text/come_ye_thankful_people_come.

[4] Some—many, it seems—do resist. It is noteworthy that Matthew tells us that "some doubted" even when the risen Jesus was right in front of them at the moment of the Great Commission (Matthew 28:17). This too, the evangelist suggests, is known to the Author of all things and does not thwart him from his purpose. Paul also faced disbelief (Romans 9–11), yet persisted even to his martyrdom. In the final analysis, the gospel cannot be suppressed, no matter how many doubters there are. What an encouragement this is to those called to mission!

[5] The "long green season" of Ordinary Time affords ample opportunity for a full development of the Old Testament background and the many episodes and teachings in the life of Christ that are introduced in Epiphany.

Coda: Doxology

[1] J. Todd Billings, *The End of the Christian Life* (Grand Rapids, MI: Brazos, 2020), 119. "End" in this context is the eschatological Greek *telos,* meaning completion, fulfillment.

[2] Thus Elijah mocked the impotence of Ba'al (1 Kings 18:27), and Isaiah makes fun of the manmade idols of Babylon (Isaiah 44:9-17).

[3] The word *ascription* is a bit awkward to define. "To ascribe" is to regard a quality as belonging to a person or thing. A dictionary definition is: to ascribe, attribute, assign, impute, or credit—meaning to lay something to the account of a person or thing. "To ascribe" suggests an inferring or conjecturing of cause, quality, authorship.

[4] I heard this every Sunday as a young person. It is indelible in my memory. I remember being very surprised—and pleased—later in life to discover it in the little-read book of Chronicles!

The Fullness of Time Series

Each volume in the Fullness of Time series invites readers to engage with the riches of the church year, exploring the traditions, prayers, Scriptures, and rituals of the seasons of the church calendar.

LENT
Esau McCaulley

ADVENT
Tish Harrison Warren

EASTER
Wesley Hill

CHRISTMAS
Emily Hunter McGowin

PENTECOST
Emilio Alvarez

EPIPHANY
Fleming Rutledge